I0061321

The Future of Television

The book is divided into two sections: one focusing on the phenomenon of television and the other on audiences. It argues that television is changing from a singular object, fixed in a particular place, to a social phenomenon distributed across many devices and platforms. It also argues that audiences are increasingly demanding an 'open relationship' with television, as their attention is often distributed across multiple devices and platforms simultaneously. In addition to these aspects, we analyse the evolution of television since its inception, the need for a renewed public service 2.0 in tune with our times, the increasing dominance of talk shows and infotainment, and the new power of television combined with artificial intelligence. These and many other topics are covered in this book, which will be of interest to television professionals, academics in sociology, media studies, and various other fields.

Abílio Almeida is Integrated Researcher at the Center for Communication and Society Studies, University of Minho, Portugal.

Routledge Advances in Sociology

For more information about this series, please visit: https://www.routledge.com/
Routledge-Advances-in-Sociology/book-series/SE0511

The Future of Television
Cultural Trajectories of Media Consumption in the Digital Age of Emotion

Abílio Almeida

Routledge
Taylor & Francis Group

LONDON AND NEW YORK

First published 2025
by Routledge
4 Park Square, Milton Park, Abingdon, Oxon OX14 4RN

and by Routledge
605 Third Avenue, New York, NY 10158

Routledge is an imprint of the Taylor & Francis Group, an informa business

© 2025 Abílio Almeida

British Library Cataloguing-in-Publication Data
A catalogue record for this book is available from the British Library

ISBN: 9781032911625 (hbk)
ISBN: 9781032911649 (pbk)
ISBN: 9781003561675 (ebk)

DOI: 10.4324/9781003561675

Typeset in Times New Roman
by KnowledgeWorks Global Ltd.

Thanks, Mum, for everything.
To list would be to reduce.

Contents

New Television, New Questions
An Introduction

Despite countless predictions to the contrary, television continues to play a significant role in numerous levels of social dynamics today. In fact, there are cases where some of the most important social figures of our time have actually risen to fame solely from television. And, what cannot be ignored is the fact that there are many others, learning from those before them, who continue to pursue this path to fame.

Moreover, there are many personalities who, despite not being experts in any particular field, recurrently appear on television. They seemingly possess opinions of great importance, which they share with the general public, often surpassing even the specialists. It is also worth noting that the largest economic and religious groups, who typically operate their own television channels, continue to rely heavily on this medium to gain visibility.

In his old book, *Praise of the General Public,* theorist Dominique Wolton (1994, p. 339) made the following statement: "yes, television is bothersome, exciting, disappointing, fascinating and tiresome". It is plausible to conclude that only a long relationship can provoke such a range of different reactions. However, it is evident that only a solid relationship can overcome negative reactions and still thrive.

In recent years, the end of television has been proclaimed time and again, but it has survived. Is it only a matter of time? Is television, especially generalist television, dying? Will the internet, social media platforms, or artificial intelligence itself eventually take over the role that television once played? Why are we seeing more programmes focused on emotion and less on ideas, whatever they may be? Are Netflix, Amazon Prime Video, HBO Max, Apple TV, Disney+, and similar platforms something different, or is television just sensitive to modern times? Will the television of the future be YouTube (traditional and short videos), Instagram (reels), TikTok, and the like? Are public service television models still relevant in today's media landscape, and is there room for a concept of Public Service 2.0 that is reimagined and more in tune with the dynamics of the modern world?

Since the beginning of the television phenomenon, one thing has been certain. Television is more than an object; it is fundamentally a social relationship

DOI: 10.4324/9781003561675-1

that not only offers but also constantly receives. However, there is one aspect of this phenomenon that has not been certain from the beginning: it is evolving. Television is becoming less a physical object in the home or in a specific physical space and more a phenomenon distributed across a variety of new and portable devices, untethered from traditional settings. This shift, unimaginable just a few years ago, also raises important and unique questions. What are the implications for the phenomenon of television? Is the long-established relationship between television and its audience changing, and if so, in what direction?

These and other questions will form the basis of the reflections that follow. But before we go any further, there is an unavoidable question: is it still useful to think about the phenomenon of television today?

Reference

Wolton, D. (1994). *[Praise of the general public: a critical theory of television] Elogio do grande público: uma teoria crítica da televisão* (M. Goucha, Trans.). Edições Asa.

Part I
Television

1 The Evolution of Television

Past, Present, and Future

1.1 We will have television in the future

"It is undeniable the existence of technical progress between [traditional] television and the internet"; however, it is also undeniable that "this technical progress is not enough for us to talk about progress in terms of communication, because the essence of this does not lie in technical performance", as Wolton (2000, p. 109, 110) said in such a straightforward way. Although managed in different ways, both have the same problem, communication in the social space, and this challenge, as Wolton suggests, is not solely reliant on technical aspects but is heavily influenced by social and cultural dimensions (p. 172).

The Internet has not killed television nor will it ever, just as modernity has not killed art. While it may be tempting to make such absolute statements, it would be unwise to do so. Art and television have both undergone transformations, much like a dying larva transforming into a butterfly. *Transformation* is the right word, not death. The new reality of the Internet has brought about a new kind of television, one that is evolving rather than dying. As Machado suggests, television is taking 'a leap towards something else' in the age of the Internet (Machado, 2011, p. 87). Echoing this idea, social theorist Miller (2009, p. 24), some years ago, said that television's reach is increasing, its flexibility is developing, its popularity is growing, and its ability to influence and incorporate both older and newer media is indisputable. Thus, television is not dead nor is it dying; it is changing.

We are undoubtedly witnessing a profound change in the television phenomenon (Faltesek et al., 2023; Johnson, 2019; Sawaia et al., 2016; Scolari, 2008; Scolari, 2009; YouGov, 2020). The rise of a new generation of users, who are well versed in interactive environments, such as video games and the Internet, has prompted television to adapt to this new digital and graphical rhetoric. Television is not dead, but its social role has changed, or at least it has a different way of connecting with society.

And we see a little of this everywhere, both in the private and public sectors: a clear concern to find a direction for television, a future for television (Casado et al., 2023; Faltesek et al., 2023; Lopes et al., 2023; Podara et al.,

DOI: 10.4324/9781003561675-3

2021; Sales, 2009; Túñez-López et al., 2021; Wayne & Sandoval, 2023). This is a clear indication that television, as a phenomenon controlled by human hands, is a part of the human future; indeed, the present also indicates that there is a future for television (CAEM/MediaMonitor, 2021; ERC, 2016; Lopes et al., 2023). From the public to the private sector, from streaming and other internet platforms to traditional television, hundreds of thousands of people across the world are now working not only on the television of today but also, more importantly, on the television of tomorrow. The question is: what kind of television will it be? And, also important is the question: how might this exploration of the future of television benefit you and others? Starting from the certainty that there will be television in our tomorrow, our main aim today is to ask questions about the apparent trajectory of television from today to tomorrow.

1.2　Think about television: What and how?

Television is a complex phenomenon with multiple intertwined paths, much like a ball of yarn. As we have seen and will later examine in more detail, it is a constantly evolving phenomenon that is influenced by numerous external forces: political, social, ideological, economic, etc. Therefore, it is impossible for a single person to analyse all the phenomena directly or indirectly associated with it. As Lopes (2009) mentioned: "studying television over time implies choosing paths" (p. 7). The question then becomes: which paths are available to the researcher?

Lopes, paraphrasing work by Corner (2003), says that there are five main areas that can be the focus of study: (1) the institution, (2) programming/realisation, (3) the sociocultural phenomenon, (4) representation and form, and (5) technology (Lopes, 2009, p. 7, 8). Although some investigations may require knowledge of more than one of these topics, it is important to remain circumscribed to an overall framework. This will facilitate not only its execution but also the interpretation by various readers. Despite the great technological advances we have seen, the five areas above seem capable of encompassing various aspects of contemporary television studies. It also seems broad enough to encompass many variables, many of which will certainly be in the future yet to come.

1.3　What is *television*: An object or a relationship?

According to Morazzo (1975), television is defined as a "telecommunications system that ensures the transmission of non-permanent images of fixed or moving objects" (p. 1232), whose main objective is to "extend the sense of vision beyond its natural limits" (p. 1232). To achieve this, it needs to "use devices capable of replacing the mechanisms of human sight, recognizing the forms and boundaries of images, understanding the distribution of light and shadows, assessing brightness and colour, and perceiving movement" (p. 1232). Based on the description by Gougenheim and d'Hérouville (2003), the term is also used to refer to "all activities related to the production and dissemination of programs" (such as when we use it to refer to public or private television), as well as to define the object itself, "the television receiver" (p. 7).

What, at its core, is television? (Wolton, 1994, p. 15). This was the question posed by one of the foremost experts in the field, Dominique Wolton, The sociologist and specialist in communication sciences offered a critical reflection on this topic, and it is worth considering his perspective, because it seems timeless.

> What, fundamentally, is television? Images and social bonding. The entertainment and the spectacle refer to the image, that is, to the technical dimension. The social bond refers to communication, that is, to the social dimension. Such is the theoretical unity of television: to associate two dimensions, technical and social, which (...) are at the origin of two great ideologies, each of them translating a disproportion in the consideration of the two dimensions. Technical ideology overvalues the role of the instrument; Political ideology, conversely, overvalues the role we can play for television. The history of television is the history of the oscillation, depending on the epochs, between each of these ideologies. This theoretical definition has the advantage of showing the essential role played by generalist television, the one that best assumes both dimensions, even if today this form of television is considered outdated.
>
> (Wolton, 1994, p. 15)

As mentioned earlier, it is important to view television not merely as an 'object' to be interpreted, but rather as a complex social 'relationship' with a dynamic of 'give and take' between both parties. From this perspective, television is fundamentally a social bond and conviviality, despite its extreme complexity and broad dimension.

Etymologically, the word television derives from the Greek *tele*, meaning distant, and from the Latin *visio*, meaning vision. This combination suggests an apparition from beyond. However, it was only in the second half of the twentieth century that this 'miracle' began, albeit very gradually, to become accessible to the general population.

Do TikTok, YouTube, and similar online platforms fit the traditional definition of television? Although they are not traditionally classified as television, we cannot ignore the fact that they meet most of the criteria of this traditional definition.

One thing is certain: to define television is to explain a social phenomenon. This requires an understanding of the society that surrounds it, so its external orientation can never be ignored. Ignoring its external orientation would be as foolish as studying someone's suffering without considering the reality that surrounds them – as warned by Bakhtin (2002, p. 99) in another context. We will therefore analyse the different phases of television, considering the different social realities. This is the only way to know how television is moving and, above all, where it seems to be going.

1.4   In the beginning there was... *paleotelevision*

According to evolutionary theory, it is believed that during the Palaeolithic period, humans distinguished themselves from other animals by starting to shape and use primitive tools such as stone. According to such a point of view, however, the real revolution came during the Neolithic period, when humans began to domesticate everything around them and become the *dominus,* the owner.

In an original text of 1983, Umberto Eco used the term, albeit somewhat ironically, "Paleotelevision" (PaleoTV) to describe the Italian television reality, which he considered to be controlling and pedagogical in nature (Eco, 1986, p. 135). He claimed that this type of television "spoke of the inaugurations of the ministers and controlled what people learn, only innocent things, even at the cost of telling lies", and that, as rudimentary as it was, "a little dictionary could be made with the names of the protagonists and the titles of the transmissions" (p. 135). Although it was Umberto Eco who created this concept, the author 'wrote little else' about it, as the researcher Lopes (2008, p. 34) said. It was later revived by theorists Casetti and Odin in their text *De la paléo- à la néo-télévision. Approche semio-pragmatique.*

According to Casetti and Odin (2012), PaleoTV takes a 'pedagogical posture' (p. 9) as its main feature, cultivating a relationship between the presenter and the viewer similar to that of the student with the teacher. This can be considered a hierarchical relationship, which incites the viewer to a clear submission. Another important feature of this type of television, from the authors' view, is the existence of a sharp border between the 'genre' (information, culture, sports, etc.) and the 'target audience' (children, the elderly, car lovers, etc.). Thus, "throughout the day, the programmes follow each other with well-marked separations" (p. 10).

> In short, in paleotelevision, the flow is subjected to a programming grid that acts fully in its structuring role. Published in the printed media, this grid allows the viewer to choose and prepare for the operations of production of meaning and affection linked to the communication contract corresponding to the chosen programme.
>
> (Casetti & Odin, 2012, p. 10)

During the PaleoTV period, the visual presentation of television was extremely rigid and constrained. In this format, it was not permitted to show numerous elements of the production to the viewer. As Eco (1986) points out that during this period, these were aspects that "should remain hidden from the public" (p. 143).

However, this would change drastically in the next phase, the Neotelevision (NeoTV) period, when such aspects would no longer be hidden but rather proudly displayed to viewers. This was because it began to be understood that this made viewers feel less deceived by television productions. One example of this was the case of applause. In NeoTV, it was no longer just any element of the production that secretly requested applause from the audience but also the presenter himself, who, without any shame, would say out loud, "and now a big round of applause!" (p. 144).

PaleoTV emerged around the 1950s and 1960s, when television was institutionalised. Due to the way it interacted with viewers, which were often distant and apathetic, it came to be perceived as boring and imperceptible, particularly as society became increasingly emotional and enthusiastic. In this context, PaleoTV was seen as too rigid for a society that prided itself on being permissive. As Casetti and Odin (2012, p. 9) suggest, this led to a general sense of frustration and disengagement among the audience, causing many to move away from it.

1.5   Which evolved into... *neotelevision*

Unlike in the PaleoTV era, where one could make a small dictionary with the names of the characters and the programme titles, NeoTV brought an end to this simplicity. As Eco (1986) observed, the number of characters and programme genres became 'infinite', with the same character taking on different roles (p. 135). This was a new television, not only in its appearance but also in its purpose. As Casetti and Odin (2012) summarise, it was no longer "a space of formation" but rather "a space of conviviality" (p. 11).

> We are certainly a long way from the pedagogical model of paleotelevision. Neotelevision is no longer an institution that is inscribed as an extension of school or family, but a place integrated into the daily space, a 'place where one lives', at least if we understand by this a place where, on both sides of the screen, there are people who spend hours and hours of their lives.
>
> (Casetti & Odin, 2012, p. 14)

In this sense, a new and attractive novelty emerged for viewers in general, drowning out the previous message: now they have the power and deserve to be continuously admired, courted, and stimulated by television itself. This is undoubtedly a new and distinct form of communication that only arose thanks to the appearance of private television. With alternatives available, it is no longer television that defines what the public sees, but rather the public that defines the television it wants to watch. "With the remote control, the public decides when to let television speak and when to move to another channel", explained the Italian theorist Umberto Eco (1986, p. 135).

If PaleoTV programmes could be compared to a primitive tool, as mentioned earlier, like a chipped stone that serves only a limited purpose, NeoTV and some of the 'new programmes' can be compared to a modern and diversified instrument, like a Swiss Army knife, bringing with it a myriad of tools and solutions. Eco (1986, p. 141), in this regard, noted that "the container programme came, where a host, perhaps for a few hours, speaks, plays music, presents a film, a documentary, a debate, and even news. At that point, even the overdeveloped viewer confuses the genres".

Casetti and Odin (2012) highlighted another crucial aspect of NeoTV, stating that "it doesn't matter if we are not experts, it doesn't matter if we completely ignore the proposed subject, the essential thing is to talk about it, the essential thing is to talk" (p. 12). As a result, there is no longer a privileged place for the cautious expert who spoke about a particular subject in the past. Instead, the place now belongs to the non-specialist who speaks proudly and without caution about everything and nothing in particular. In short, NeoTV presents itself as an amplification of everyday chatter of life (p. 12).

According to Eco (1986), NeoTV created a greater connection with many adults through the use of ulterior motives and expletives (p. 149). This is a new kind of television, in which presenters and guests are on first-name terms, patting each other on the back, and constantly laughing and joking (Casetti & Odin, 2012, p. 13). The presenter is no longer a distant and impeccable teacher as in PaleoTV, but a peer who is impulsive, flawed, and tolerant. In this sense, the popular knowledge of the common citizen, and those who best reflect it, are privileged, and specialised knowledge is gradually relegated to the background. As some authors have suggested, the *truth* becomes a secondary issue on television, and the most crucial aspect is that it *truly communicates*.

NeoTV, which emerged predominantly in the last two decades of the twentieth century, reflected an increasingly deepening crisis of modern society. This crisis, according to theorist Lourenço (2006), was primarily a 'crisis of values', indicating a growing societal struggle to define what is or is not common sense based on its own criteria.

Rather than attracting viewers through sound arguments, television increasingly sought to provide emotional stimulation. The limit of this symptom of the times became increasingly contested, as the relationship between viewer and television was no longer based on shared ideas but on shared meanings and a harmony of emotions. Thus, NeoTV can be seen as the era of 'sensitisation' of television.

1.6 And then came... *hypertelevision*

Subtly departing from the concepts initiated by Eco (1986) and Casetti and Odin (2012), the sociologist Verón (2009) suggested that, with the turn of the century, a new third stage in the history of television for the general public had begun (p. 17). He argued that the introduction of reality shows is a clear indication of the beginning of this third stage (p. 18), in which ordinary citizens of the world have become 'consecrated', that is, *televisible*; although external to the television institution, they have come to be shaped and 'offered' by it. This new phase offers a hybrid reality that is both real and fictitious for those who observe it – a truly empathetic 'offering' made with some chosen members of the audience. Aladro (2000) noted that this has led to a new way of watching television, where the main objective of viewers is to "examine human behaviour and discuss it" (p. 292).

Contrary to many assumptions, television has not become just that, but over time, also that. This observation was made by Lopes (2008), who noted that while audiences were drawn to the new reality shows, most of the programmes on generalist channels still excluded the public (p. 45). As a result, Lopes proposed a new concept that marked a different stage but was still transitional in nature, called 'post-neo-television' (p. 45).

Another researcher who proposed a new television reality is Scolari (2008) in his work titled *Towards hypertelevision. The first symptoms of a new configuration of the television device*. He called this new phase 'hypertelevision', a type of television that he says is a by-product of the times. It is directed towards users who are used to interacting with various digital media, such as the Internet and games. He suggests that television is not dying, but rather, it is restructuring its role as the backbone of society (p. 7).

Indeed, it is impossible not to notice that in the last few years, there has been a significant leap in the progress associated with television devices. If PaleoTV reflected the era of television monopolies and NeoTV marked the birth of private television, the upcoming new television will undoubtedly continue to be a unique reflection of the society that surrounds it. *Surfing* the television is becoming more and more like surfing the Internet, and there's no denying that (Esler, 2021). And there is also no denying that interacting with television is increasingly similar to interacting with our smartphones and computers.

There were those who doubted Scolari's statements (2008), myself included, but even though his 'prophecy' was several years old, it is undeniable that he was a visionary. Much of what he said now makes perfect sense. And if TikTok, YouTube, and the like fit the traditional definition of television to some extent, they will undoubtedly fit it even better with this update. An update that continues, as the next section will analyse.

1.7   Which gave a long future to... *ubiquitous television*

The word 'ubiquitous', from the Latin *ubique,* describes something that is present everywhere. It is synonymous with the words such as 'omnipresent' or 'universal'. Therefore, it is then understood that when we talk about 'Ubiquitous Television', we are referring to a kind of television that, regardless of the time and place, is fully available and accessible to its audience – that is, 24 hours a day, 7 days a week, 365 days a year. Ubiquity is a concept that not only applies to the television phenomenon but also extends to the most varied and distinct means of communication. However, as is to be expected, in the reflection that follows, we will give special attention to issues that are related to television either directly or indirectly.

Until not so long ago, much of television content was available only in the kitchen, living room, bedroom, or other physical room. And whether in a public or private setting, these contents remained accessible only for a limited period of time. In order for the desired programmes to be viewed, viewers had to adjust not only their programming to the television channel but also move to the location of the television. However, with the changes that have taken place in the recent past, this reality has changed. Today, for a significant number of users, television content is available in our pockets (on mobile phones), and, regardless of the time or place, it remains just a few clicks away. As the researcher Filho (2015) points out, 'the environment that was characterised by the condition of seeing at a distance establishes with digital technology another reality: to be seen everywhere' (p. 101). In this specific field, it is also no longer possible to deny that we are witnessing a reinterpretation – another one – of what has hitherto been regarded as the phenomenon of television.

This is largely due to the emergence of various mobile devices with a good capacity to play audiovisual content, such as smartphones and tablets, as well as the increasingly wide and easier access to the Internet for a very significant number of users. In view of all these transformations, it is therefore understandable that not only the theoretical concept once used should be the subject of a new and broader reflection but also that a number of other practical aspects need a new understanding (Dawson, 2010; Es, 2023; Faltesek et al., 2023).

For the researcher Correia (2015), there are several challenges that will involve the new television. Based on his reflection, we believe that the first challenge will be regarding creativity and being able to adapt the content to new environments. The second will be related to the increasingly close coexistence between television and social networks. This will encompass a new sort of exposure to a greater public dimension, which will be either appreciated or criticised by users. Consequently, there is a greater need to provide rapid, constant, and adequate explanations. The next challenge will be that of discourse and the possible need to adapt it to a new media environment. This may also lead to the creation of new hybrid genres. The final challenge, which is directly related to the other points, will be around the business model itself. Despite the challenges, one thing is certain: in order to survive, television producers must find solutions to share content. Your very 'life' depends on uninterrupted content sharing. However, who can truly guarantee its existence? In *Television in its labyrinth*, Gradim (2015) notes that the television industry is currently at a crossroads. But, as the title suggests, it is its crossroads, its labyrinth. Therefore, it is reasonable to ask that television professionals, who orchestrate, regulate, and examine it, seek, create, and find solutions. In fact, some changes are already underway and cannot be ignored.

Content that was once only viewed in the comfort of our homes can now be seen during a train ride, on a bus, and in other settings. These factors, among others, obviously need to be considered when designing content because they affect how well it is absorbed and understood. For these and other reasons, the audience appears to be increasingly distracted, causing a decline in the popularity of dense content which requires reasonable attention from viewers. On the other hand, entertainment or infotainment, a hybrid genre that some believe blends information with entertainment, is gaining popularity.

Even in so-called traditional live television, it is increasingly important to consider the many comments posted by viewers on social media. Unlike in the recent past, these evaluations often have an immediate impact on the programme. This reality encourages everyone involved to be prepared to deal with unexpected issues and to improvise on any topic that arises. As a result, programmes become more unpredictable and emotional. Once aired, however, these often-long programmes still need to be broken down into smaller topics with short titles and subtitles so that web users can easily absorb them on social media or on the programme or channel's own website.

Although, as previously discussed, ubiquity is a broader concept in the context of the television industry. Considering its history, we believe that it is likely just another change in the evolution of television. This change may have initially caused some internal restlessness, but it will ultimately make television more resilient externally. To sum up, the 'great mirror' that was once in the bedroom, living room, or kitchen is now broken into smaller pieces, residing in the pockets of viewers. Symbolically, we refer to this as 'Ubiquitous Television', represented by a portable, *pocket mirror* that allows viewers to access *their* own image and imagination at any time and in any place.

This, therefore, seems to be the path of modern television, the television of tomorrow. It is above all in these areas that its space for technological and social progress seems to be emerging in the coming years. However, we cannot deny that this television is already here. In a way, we can say that the future has largely arrived, or rather, has already begun to arrive.

As a human, social, and technological phenomenon, television seems to be moving towards being less and less a specific technological object and more and more a social phenomenon, diluted in many other objects of a technological nature. It is now less an object of communication and more a phenomenon of communication than it was in the past. And in recent years, this seems to be the great secret of television's survival as a phenomenon. And it seems to be where its future lies.

References

Aladro, E. (2000). [From soap opera to tele-vigilance. "Big Brother" and the new era of relational perspectivism on television] De la telenovela a lo televigilancia. "GranHermano" y la nueva era del perspectivismo relacional en la televisión. *Cuadernos de Información y Comunicación, 5,* 291–300. http://revistas.ucm.es/index.php/CIYC/article/view/CIYC0000110291A

Bakhtin, M. (2002). *[Questions of literature and aesthetics] Questões de literatura e de estética* (A. Bernardini, J. Júnior, A. Júnior, H. Nazário, H. Andrade, Trans.; 5th ed.). Editora Hucitec/Annablume.

CAEM/MediaMonitor. (2021). Total TV 2020 (YUMI Analytics Desktop).

Casado, M., Guimerà, J., Bonet, M., & Llavador, J. (2023). Adapt or die? How traditional Spanish TV broadcasters deal with the youth target in the new audiovisual ecosystem. *Critical Studies in Television, 18*(3), 256–273. https://doi.org/10.1177/17496020221076983

Casetti, F., & Odin, R (2012). From Paleo to Neotelevision: Semiopragmatic approach] Da Paleo à Neotelevisão: abordagem semiopragmática. *Ciberlegenda, 27,* 8–22.

Corner, J. (2003). Finding data, reading patterns, telling stories: issues in the historiography of television. *Media, Culture & Society, 25*(2), 273–280. https://doi.org/10.1177/01634437030252006

Correia, J. C. (2015). [Ubiquity: The next television revolution] Ubiquidade: A próxima revolução televisiva. In P. Serra, S. Sá, W. S. Filho (Eds.), *A Televisão Ubíqua* (pp. 39–52). LabCom. http://www.labcom-ifp.ubi.pt/livro/136

Dawson, M. (2010). Television between analog and digital. *Journal of Popular Film and Television, 38*(2), 95–100. https://doi.org/10.1080/01956051.2010.483361

Eco, U. (1986). *[Journey into everyday unreality] Viagem na irrealidade quotidiana* (M. Pinto, Trans.). Difel.

ERC. (2016). *[The new dynamics of audiovisual consumption in Portugal] As novas dinâmicas do consumo audiovisual em Portugal.* ERC.

Es, K. V. (2023). Netflix & Big Data: The strategic ambivalence of an entertainment company. *Television & New Media, 24*(6), 656–672. https://doi.org/10.1177/15274764221125745

Esler, M. (2021). In plain sight: Online TV interfaces as branding. *Television & New Media, 22*(7), 727–742. https://doi.org/10.1177/1527476420917104

Faltesek, D., Graalum, E., Breving, B., Knudsen, E., Lucas, J., Young, S., & Zambrano, F. (2023). TikTok as television. *Social Media + Society, 9*(3). https://doi.org/10.1177/20563051231194576

Filho, W. S. (2015). [The influence of technology in the transformation of television in the 21st century] A influência da tecnologia na transformação da televisão no século XXI. In P. Serra, S. Sá, W. S. Filho (Eds.), *A Televisão Ubíqua* (pp. 83–104). LabCom. http://www.labcom-ifp.ubi.pt/livro/136

Gougenheim, I., & d'Hérouville, Y. (2003). *[The television] A televisão* (A. Rodrigues, Trans.). Editorial Inquérito.

Gradim, A. (2015). [Television in its labyrinth] A televisão no seu labirinto. In P. Serra, S. Sá, W. S. Filho (Eds.), *A Televisão Ubíqua* (pp. 69–82). LabCom. http://www.labcom-ifp.ubi.pt/livro/136

Johnson, C. (2019). *Online TV.* Routledge.

Lopes, F. (2008). [From post-neo-television: The reconfiguration of prime-time in Portuguese generalist channels] Da pós-neotelevisão: a reconfiguração do prime-time nos canais generalistas portugueses. In M. Pinto, S. Marinho (Eds.), *Os media em Portugal nos primeiros cinco anos do século XXI* (pp. 33–46). Campo das Letras.

Lopes, F. (2009). [Television studies: diachronic perspectives] Estudos televisivos: perspectivas diacrónicas. *Comunicação e Sociedade, 15*, 7–27. https://doi.org/10.17231/comsoc.15(2009).1042

Lopes, F., Burnay, C., Santos, C., Santos, F., Wemans, J., Romano, R., & Silva, S. G. d. (2023). *[Public media service - White Paper] Serviço público de média - Livro branco.* Ministério da Educação e Ciência.

Lourenço, E. (2006). [In the shadow of Nietzsche] À sombra de Nietzsche. In C. d. Sousa, J. d. Lima (Eds.), *Heterodoxias* (Vol. 1). Fundação Calouste Gulbenkian.

Machado, A. (2011). End of television. *Fim da televisão? Famecos, 18*(1), 86–97. doi: https://doi.org/10.15448/1980-3729.2011.1.8799.

Miller, T. (2009). [Television is over, television has become a thing of the past, television is gone] A televisão acabou, a televisão virou coisa do passado, a televisão já era (V. Purper, Trans.). In J. F. Filho (Ed.), *A TV em transição: tendências de programação no Brasil e no mundo* (pp. 9–25).

Morazzo, L. (1975). [Television] Televisão. In *Enciclopedia Luso Brasileira Da Cultura* (1st ed., Vol. 17, pp. 1232–1239). Verbo.

Podara, A., Matsiola, M., Kotsakis, R., Maniou, T., & Kalliris, G. (2021). Generation Z's screen culture: Understanding younger users' behaviour in the television streaming age - The case of post-crisis Greece. *Critical Studies in Television, 16*(2), 91–109. https://doi.org/10.1177/17496020211005395

Sales, M. (2009). The future of television: from the boob tube to YouTube. *American Communication Journal, 11*(1).

Sawaia, J., Juliasz, F., Crippa, T., & Kakazu, K. (2016). The television consumption journey in different platforms in the Era of Liquid Content. *Brazilian Journal of Marketing, 9*(3), 192–212. https://revistapmkt.com.br/pt_br/categoria/publicacoes/2016/

Scolari, C. A. (2008). [Towards hypertelevision. The first symptoms of a new configuration of the television device] Hacia la hipertelevisión. Los primeros síntomas de una nueva configuración del dispositivo televisivo. *Diálogos de la comunicación, 77.*, 1–9.

Scolari, C. A. (2009). The grammar of hypertelevision: An identikit of convergence-age fiction television (or, how television simulates new interactive media). *Journal of Visual Literacy, 28*(1), 28–50. https://doi.org/10.1080/23796529.2009.11674658

Túñez-López, M., Campos-Freire, F., & Rodríguez-Castro, M. (Eds.). (2021). *The values of public service media in the internet society.* Palgrave Macmillan.

Verón, E (2009). Publics between production and reception: Problems for a theory of recognition] Os públicos entre produção e recepção: problemas para uma teoria do reconhecimento. *Eco-Pós, 12*(1), 11–26. doi: https://doi.org/10.29146/eco-pos.v12i1.965.

Wayne, M., & Sandoval, A (2023). Netflix original series, global audiences and discourses of streaming success. *Critical Studies in Television, 18*(1), 81–100. doi: https://doi.org/10.1177/17496020211037259.

Wolton, D. (1994). *[Praise of the general public: A critical theory of television] Elogio do grande público: uma teoria crítica da televisão* (M. Goucha, Trans.). Edições Asa.

Wolton, D. (2000). *[And after the Internet? Towards a critical theory of new media] E depois da internet? Para uma teoria crítica dos novos médias* (R. Branco, Trans.). Difel.

YouGov. (2020). One in eight people watch TV on their phone each day. *YouGov.* https://yougov.co.uk/technology/articles/32766-one-eight-people-watch-tv-their-phone-each-day

2 The New Television
Old Ideas in a New World

2.1 Public and private solutions: With a goal that never goes out of fashion

The concept of public service, which also extends to radio and other media, has – or should have (as we will analyse later) – the fundamental goal of serving the public interest. While this might seem straightforward, it inevitably raises important questions such as who can serve and how best to serve the public interest. Before we delve into this complex debate, let us begin with a brief history of public service television, starting from its beginning.

According to Fidalgo (2005), the creation of the BBC in the United Kingdom in 1926 marked the beginning of public service and served, to a large extent, as a pioneering model for the rest of Europe. Fidalgo identifies several key principles that underpin public service television, including *universality*, which seeks to bring high-quality television to all citizens; *diversity*, which aims to inform, educate, and entertain viewers; *public financing*, which holds the government accountable for providing financial support; and, controversially, *independence*, which requires television to be free from governmental and private interests (p. 24). These principles, among others, clearly distinguish public service from private or commercial television, as shown in Table 2.1. The table is based on the classic model. However, it also seems to apply, with reasonable assertiveness, to what are still today the two main media models (public and private) and their respective roles and visions in society.

It is worth noting that, unlike the United States of America, which emerged from World War II with a strengthened political system, most European countries were left in a weakened state. As a result, state television on this side of the Atlantic played a crucial role in trying to "restore consensus and national identity" (Bustamante, 2003, p. 32), particularly in the wake of devastating conflicts like the Second World War. At that time, according to Fidalgo (2005, p. 24), state television was an essential connection between the state and the nation, promoting national identity through political, linguistic, and cultural means.

DOI: 10.4324/9781003561675-4

Table 2.1 The public and commercial models

	Public	Commercial
Role of the State	Managing State	State arbitrator
Ensuring pluralism	Public management	Market (competition)
Financing	Rate	Advertising
Dominant dynamics	Politics/Culture	Economy/Politics
Programmatic objectives	Information/Education/ Entertainment	Entertainment
Production	Own-National	Multiple (Own/Other) (Domestic/Imported)
Addressee	Citizen	Consumer
Legitimacy	Satisfaction (Weight of audience)	Quantity (Fidelity)

Source: Based on Bustamante (2003, p. 37).

Later, around the 1980s and 1990s, with the emergence of private television, the public service experienced a broad and multifaceted crisis. According to Bustamante (2003, pp. 60–62), three important areas in which this crisis flourished are:

• *Economic and financial field:* Financial revenues fell due to multiple factors, while the number of hours of broadcasting was forced to increase to cope with the new private channels. As a result, expenses also increased and were greater than revenues.
• *Political front:* States and governments deprived the public service of the means to cope with new and severe competition.
• *Socio-cultural field:* The public began to choose private televisions in general, which were filled with entertainment. As a result, advertising revenues declined, and governments further curbed public funds.

In general, the emergence of private television left (so-called) public service televisions with two options: maintain their social identity or compete directly with private television. A large part, according to Bustamante (2003), "given the fall of resources and audiences, ended up falling into the trap choosing the second option and thus closing the vicious circle of their own loss of legitimacy" (p. 63). The 'war' between public and private service television, according to Wolton (1994, pp. 25–32), can be broken down into three periods:

1 *1950–1970: The dominance of the public service television model.* The priority is educational and popular programmes, but politically controlled;
2 *1970–1980: The confrontation between the two models.* The erosion of the politically controlled public television model is becoming increasingly remarkable.
3 *1980–1990: The turnaround.* Private television is a must. Public television tries to disconnect from politics.

Before examining what public service should be, according to some authors, it is important to understand what private television represents in today's economic reality. Firstly, it is crucial to not be blinded by the constant philanthropic discourse of private television as it aims to achieve maximum investment in advertising and, like any other company in a capitalist society, to maximise profits, as highlighted by Bustamante (2003, p. 75). This results in viewers being primarily viewed as mere consumers of a product. Until this product becomes visible, the producer, like any private company, faces numerous internal and external challenges. These include the need to think ahead of something that can generate large audiences (so that advertising time is valued more) and the need to consider the intense and fierce competition (Bustamante, 2003).

It is not uncommon to witness an 'anything goes' attitude from private media companies in pursuit of higher audience ratings and profits. Unfortunately, this approach can lead to a disregard for the well-being of citizens and the broader public interest. As researcher Sousa (1999) warned, "private television can, with all legitimacy, aim at profit. It cannot, however, do so at any cost" (p. 125). Of course, the general public interest should be above any particular economic interest. But is this what happens in practice? This is an important question that, with its ups and downs, continues to be the subject of ongoing discussion.

It is clear that both public and private services have the potential and responsibility to serve the public interest. However, while private television is obligated to meet the minimum legal requirements, public service television should aim to go above and beyond to serve the public. This difference in character and motivation is what sets public service apart and gives it its unique identity. As Fidalgo (2005, p. 37) summarises, public service is not simply a function that can be turned 'on' or 'off' according to programming or audience, but rather a permanent identity that must be understood and upheld by the legislator and the channel administration. Although private services can occasionally provide a public service, public service must always prioritise the public interest above all else.

Thus, public service is not merely expected to provide a public service on occasion, as other private channels may also purport to do. Instead, it is expected to do so consistently and continuously, with the provision of public service being its primary and defining objective. Public service is expected to act with exemplary conduct and produce content of exceptional quality in all areas in which it operates, distinguishing itself not through quantity but through the high quality of its output.

To fully comprehend the fundamental contrast between public and private services, one must analyse two distinct and completely opposite perspectives of television's relationship with the society it serves. According to Pinto (2005b, p. 42), these views reflect the role of the media in different visions of society: commercial perceives the audience as a market and its members as consumers, while public service perceives them as members of a community. The primary goal of the former is to benefit the internal institution, while the latter focuses on external benefits, which in this case refers to the well-being of the country and its society.

In order to operate in the public sphere, media companies must comply with the legal rules that this space requires, depending on the country or region. And the permanent orientation towards the public interest is undoubtedly the goal that both solutions (public or private/commercial) should have. But what future do these old ideas and values have in this new (media) world? We will try to answer this next.

2.2   The so-called public service, the public service, and a public service 2.0 for the future?

Public service television asserts itself and differentiates itself by its character of reference and exemplarity. Instead of levelling down, it sets the bar as high as possible in terms of professionalism, the specificities of television discourse and aesthetics, the ability to arouse interest and broaden horizons. It does not embark on a minimalist policy that is limited to the minimums that the law provides.

(Pinto, 2005a, p. 16)

In order to fulfil its purpose, public service should strive for excellence without mistaking style for elitism or excessive seriousness. As Pinto (2005a, p. 16) cautions, television should not confine itself to specific forms and styles, seriousness, or exclusivity towards any particular genre. Lopes (1999) believes the public should be committed to offering programmes that are diverse at regional, political, and cultural levels. But not only to serve the public, but also to be made with the public. Pinto (2005b) claimed that public service television's existence would make 'no sense' (p. 49) without active public participation. Despite the difficulties of our times, it is expected to be continuously "an open window against exclusion, contributing to the social and cultural integration of society" (Brandão, 2006, p. 20) rather than a closed mirror. This open window must exist as a place of resistance, dissent, and creativity, as Martins (2005) puts it, to justify its presence.

In light of what many believe and what has been analysed, we can see that public service has a different purpose. It fights, but not solely for financial gain, and uses different weapons. We are talking about a solution that, instead of viewing the audience as mere consumers, sees them, above all, as important citizens. This idea of media solutions emphasises societal well-being, rowing against the current of capitalism. As Fidalgo (2005, p. 39) explains, the existence of public service is only warranted when it possesses distinctiveness, autonomy, and a unique identity in comparison to other available options.

In this follow-up, according to researchers Gonçalves and Pires (2005), advertising should not "be seen as a hindrance and an enemy to be slaughtered (…), [because] it would be interesting to take advantage of its persuasive power and its modelling form of behaviours to trigger the process of full adherence to the values of citizenship" (p. 129). Moreover, in the authors' opinion, "advertising … should be [also] considered as a form of financing" (p. 129), although obviously with some limits. This perspective recognises advertising as a modern tool and expands the range of legitimate tools for public service media. Instead of simply removing advertising, the goal is to use it in conjunction with other means to benefit society and promote its well-being.

Based on the aspects analysed so far, we can conclude that public media must not be detached from social reality but rather be constantly attentive and sensitive to the society that surrounds it. It should aim to satisfy large social groups while also creating content for minorities. This is undoubtedly a challenging task, but it is only through its constant execution that the existence of public service media can be justified.

Although today's public service television has evolved from what was once called Paleotelevision (PaleoTV), it still has a crucial role to play in 'educating' and 'serving' the citizens. According to Pinto (2005a), "it is legitimate to expect from a television that is guided by service to citizens that takes into account, in its strategic decisions and in the options of a conjunctural nature, the needs and asymmetries of the 'real country'"(p. 17). Similarly, Brandão (2006, p. 20) emphasises the importance of public television's formative, cultural, and ethical role.

Although the reality was very different in the 90s and 00s, today there seem to be signs of improvement everywhere. The public service was linked to and served the political powers (Martins, 2005; Sousa & Santos, 2005; Torres, 2011; Vasconcelos, 2003). It was often a public service in name only, serving primarily the political power that governed. Today, there is a clear improvement in the area of independence. However, other problems of a different nature still seem to haunt the public service media.

There is an urgent need for a more 'digitalised' public service. A new, renewed public service, more sensitive to the world around it. This does not mean 'diminishing' the fundamental values that characterise it. We are therefore talking about the importance of transformation, or rather rejuvenation while maintaining the same basic principles (Lopes et al., 2023; Túñez-López et al., 2021). If it is necessary not to lose the direction that has defined the values of public service, it is also important to consider the new surrounding environment (social, economic, and technological). Based on these two points, we can think about moving towards a new and renewed public service that is increasingly closer to the people, that is, increasingly 'digitalised' (Es & Poell, 2020; Lopes et al., 2023).

Based on the information presented in this topic, it is clear that public service television should not be regarded as a minor form of television, but rather as a different type of television (Pinto, 2005b). In essence, public television should not view its audience as mere consumers or potential voters but as important citizens of a community.

Again, do these core values that underpin public service change with new times and new media technologies? Of course not. And why not? They are the compass, regardless of the terrain and atmosphere in which one is navigating (Lopes et al., 2023; Túñez-López et al., 2021). Public services seem to be changing (Donders, 2019; Lopes et al., 2023), increasingly comfortable in the new digital world, on the Internet and social media, but not yet fully comfortable, not as much as private institutions seem to be. There is room for improvement, and they should work in this direction. Is there an alternative to this adaptation? Certainly not.

It is therefore imperative to develop a new set of public service solutions that are in line with both traditional values and modern advances for the digital age. We are talking about a renewed public service, a kind of Public Service 2.0, where the old values are adapted to our times and the times to come, and where the remembrance of the 'values of citizenship' will undoubtedly be very useful, as it is today.

2.3   A war with (no)future: The generalist, thematic, streaming, and personal solutions

Television programming is becoming increasingly fragmented with each passing day. Unlike in the past, nowadays, we have access to hundreds of channels that allow us to watch content based on our personal preferences and interests, be it sports, music, culture, religion, or even more niche programming associated with a specific sports team, cultural organisation, or religious group. While it is clear that a channel exists because it has an audience that watches it, what is not immediately apparent is that the channel also depends on that audience's ability to pay for it, directly or indirectly – a feat that requires a significant number of subscribers.

There are various factors that led to the rise of traditional fragmented television, as explained by sociologist Wolton (1994). He identifies four fundamental reasons for this phenomenon. The first reason is technological progress, which has made it easier and more affordable to access and produce programmes. The second reason is the fragmentation of the television audience, as people have become more specific in their viewing preferences, being no longer satisfied by the openness offered by generalist television. The third reason is the emergence of a competitive market with more companies offering high-quality audiovisual content. Finally, the fourth reason is the decline of generalist television, which has become unappealing to many viewers over time (pp. 116–119).

Although there has been much written about the emergence of fragmented television, generalist television has continued to thrive, to the surprise of many. One of the main reasons for its success is its diversified and broad nature, which guarantees a more comprehensive market and allows for maximum profits. In addition to the economic benefits, Wolton adds that generalist television serves as a "factor of social integration and collective identity" by providing a large-scale gathering at the national level (p. 126). Wolton also notes other factors that have contributed to its success, such as the relationship between information and the various programmes that express in generalist television the true and diversified social reality, the nature of programming that allows viewers to choose popular programmes, and the sense of community and bond it provides among viewers (pp. 127–131).

It appears that irrespective of the existence of generalist television, society will always have the need to come together in large gatherings. Therefore, this comprehensive and diverse television solution, while offering diversity also unavoidably provides uniformity, only serves as a space to satisfy a human and social need. Torres (2011) points out the fact that liking a programme is often dependent on whether viewers watch it with someone else or share it (p. 39). Thus, from this perspective, generalist television can be seen as a form of 'social cement' (p. 40), something unifying. An emotional connection that is now extended to a global level with the new streaming TV platforms, because we can share and talk about what we are watching not only with people in our country but with people all over the world, in person or on social media platforms because it is a global offering.

On the other hand, smaller gatherings, either at specific times for some or regularly for others, are also essential. And it is these 'specific needs' that fragmented TV will continue to meet, whether temporarily or not. Something similar is happening with personal online channels (YouTube, Instagram, TikTok, etc.), where many of them, especially some of the most popular ones, are now super developed, both in terms of graphics and content. And, of course, many of them have more resources than traditional thematic channels.

This dynamic, with respect to its division, in some ways brings us closer to the concept of tribes by the sociologist Maffesoli (1998). Traditional fragmented television and the new personal channels on Internet platforms often reproduce audiovisual content for a limited group of people who share the same linguistic characteristics, dress similarly, and have similar interests. This creates a sense of community around something specific. This can be surfing, gaming, climbing, travelling, and an almost infinite number of other possibilities.

Contrary to popular belief, there does not seem to be an open war between these various new or old solutions. It is not uncommon to see professionals from generalist channels promoting programmes from thematic channels or even from their personal online channels (YouTube, Instagram, TikTok, etc.). Often what is briefly mentioned on generalist TV serves as a teaser for the more focused programmes on fragmented/thematic TV. And many of the programmes that become popular on streaming platforms can later be found on generalist or thematic channels, and vice versa. And many traditional media companies that grew up with traditional TV are now developing their streaming platforms – something that also 'affects' public service across Europe (Lopes et al., 2023).

In each of the solutions, whether regional or global, amateur or professional, whether a national football team match or a neighbour's live broadcast on social media, what we see in this dilution of the new television is the same as in the past. A gathering of people to see something in common, to feel something in common.

So, it seems clear that the television of the future is moving towards being more of a media solution, diluted in many other technological solutions, rather than something static, tied to a single technological solution. But now we are going to analyse an increasingly common element in the four content solutions discussed in this topic: the talk show. Why are they everywhere? That is the question we will try to answer.

2.4   The (emotional) talk shows: The content of the past with more future?

There are more and more talk shows. They are not only on traditional TV but also on so-called modern TV: they are everywhere on streaming platforms and on the Internet (especially on YouTube channels or similar). Some people might say it is just because it is cheap to do a talk show, but is that the only reason? It is certainly a factor that can contribute a lot. But not only that. Talk shows – or rather the nature of talk shows – seem to fit perfectly into the social reality we live in today. But first of all, it seems important to understand its nature.

Firstly, it is important to distinguish any debate or conversation from a talk show. Timberg (2002, p. 3) stated, "the television *talk show*, as opposed to *television talk*, is the television show that is entirely structured around the act of conversation itself." In other words, the conversation – not the topic – is the main element of the programme, and everything revolves around it. This means that, unlike other formats where conversation is just one part of many, talk shows are specifically designed to showcase conversation.

Viewed from this perspective, it is reasonable to conclude that although there may be numerous and diverse discussions within any talk show, one cannot assume the existence of a talk show within many of the varied debates. Therefore, it is important to note that a talk show is much more than just 'small talk', as it involves presenting a show – primarily centred around the act of talking – about a particular theme. For the show to remain engaging, it is often necessary to incorporate various ingredients, including those from the realms of information, entertainment, reality, or fiction.

According to Charaudeau and Ghiglione (2000), there are several aspects that distinguish and characterise the talk show. The authors highlight four of these essential aspects (pp. 104–106): firstly, the opinions and emotions of each participant are made public. Secondly, It is a discursive cheating that is revealed in its own staging. The talk show functions only as a discourse of the moment, without origin, without memory, which intends to reveal the hidden and finally appears naked, without truth, without any riddle to solve. Thirdly, the talk show aims to make heard and display the opinion of a 'me' that actually wants and aims to mean a 'we' – as broad as possible, resuming an inevitable and intrinsic question associated with the television phenomenon as a social 'mirror'. Fourth. The talk show is a spectacle of the word, where, although in theory they are usually distinguished by themes, in practice, themes are often mixed: the issues of the public domain with those of the private domain, what is serious with what is fun, etc.

Based on the aforementioned authors' explanation, the talk show is a paradoxical genre that is presented as being in a contract of interaction with the viewer, yet the viewer is ultimately disconnected from the process, resulting in what the authors call "the ideology of the simulacrum" (p. 106). The talk show is not simply an exercise in dialogue but rather a spectacle that requires the addition of conflict, drama, and emotions to maintain viewer interest (p. 97). Moreover, the talk show serves as a means to provoke the viewer's sense of identity and empathy, aligning it with the broader appeal of reality shows (p. 147). Thus, the talk show is not only a form of entertainment but also a reflection of the social and cultural values of the time – a very particular time in which the *truth* has become secondary, and the most important aspect is to *truly communicate*. The enthusiasm, the passion, and the wide range of emotions with which people communicate seem increasingly to be more important than *what* those people communicate. This increasingly seems to be the media reality of the present, and therefore the media reality that is increasingly being predicted for the future.

Talk shows occupy a middle ground between programmes that entertain and those that inform. Despite having been around for several decades, today they are ubiquitous and can be found at any time. While in the past, talk shows were primarily associated with information, nowadays, they are increasingly linked to entertainment. This shift reflects the current times, characterised by a new social regime that prioritises fun and infantilisation (Lipovetsky, 2007; Maffesoli, 2001, 2014). Television and its programming have adapted to this new reality, which has affected the talk show genre as well. It begs the question: is the talk show genre a form of 'revenge' of popular knowledge against the once-revered official knowledge? If the answer is yes, this is not surprising, as it is a longstanding symptom of (post) modernism.

If talk shows have occupied a significant space in the past and continue to do so today, all the signs are that they will occupy even more space in the future. Increasingly, however, the focus seems to be on emotions rather than ideas – in effect, they are becoming more and more emotional shows disguised as talk shows.

2.5   Infotainment: The next entertainment or information?

The term 'information' has its roots in the Latin word *informare*, which means 'to give form'. This is still relevant today, as the same 'truth' can take different forms depending on who is modelling it for the public. On the other hand, 'entertainment' is derived from the French word *entretenir*, which means 'to have between', suggesting a crucial role in bridging the main elements. In the early days of television, or PaleoTV, information was the primary element of programming, with entertainment serving as a way to soften and connect the rest of the content. However, over time, this has shifted, and entertainment has become the primary and sustaining pillar of television programming, with information taking on a secondary role.

Many programmes today are considered to belong to the category of 'infotainment'. This term refers to shows that exist somewhere between the traditional realm of information and pure entertainment. However, the exact definition of 'infotainment' remains a pertinent question. Drawing on Brants (1998, p. 327) explanation, it can be suggested that infotainment is located in a middle ground between the 'serious side', which aims to provide objective information where the message is more important than the image, and the 'entertainment side', where the focus on image, spectacle, and emotions can mask the underlying message. For the author, this genre combines aspects of political information in entertainment programmes or entertainment aspects in programmes that are traditionally information.

According to Stockwell's reflection (2004), infotainment can be viewed as a 'bag' that contains various styles, formats, or subgenres. The only common characteristic among them is that they fall somewhere between the two main pillars of television: information and entertainment (p. 2). He refers to something that has a hybrid nature and an ability to 'feed' from various sources almost simultaneously. Something that can be compared to a kind of octopus. As the author points out, it is something that can "spread its tentacles in both directions" (p. 7), thus gathering whatever it desires, whether it be information or entertainment, depending on whatever its current 'appetite' might be.

When reflecting on the concept today, another inevitable question arises: whether it is information that aims to entertain or entertainment that aims to inform. And this new dilemma seems to surround virtually all media content at the moment. There are a myriad of issues contributing to this structural social change, which, while not being directly related to television itself, are at the heart of this structural social change, as mentioned earlier. However, television programming has also mirrored this new reality, as it is part of its nature. This shift has been referred to as Neotelevision by many. As a result, informative and entertainment content, which were once distinct, have increasingly become part of the same package. Programmes no longer belong solely to the realms of pure information or pure entertainment, but rather they both entertain and inform. But what should we expect in the future: entertainment more closely linked to information, or information more closely linked to entertainment?

In fact, this separation from reality is becoming increasingly difficult. And it is likely to become even more so in the future. For example, even the most traditional TV news programmes – which serve as a model for the entire media landscape around the world – are now incorporating more and more of what used to be entertainment. What about mainstream entertainment? It seems to be focusing more and more on delivering messages that used to be in the realm of 'information'.

What is the challenge that we face today and that will be even greater in the future? To recognise what is pure entertainment and what is pure information; to understand the messages behind the noise; to extract emotions from the information; to absorb the pure information; and then, if we wish, to add our own emotions based on our personal and social experience.

2.6 What kind of future can we expect?

Television, which once served the purpose of showcasing the unimaginable and diverse aspects of the world we live in, acting as an open window to the world, now seems to be increasingly focused on reflecting the *ideal* of each individual and showcasing it incessantly in its numerous and diverse programmes and characters. The ultimate goal is clear: to evoke emotions in the viewer that lead to an empathetic relationship with what is being seen and heard, and above all, with the human mediator of that content. If television was once more focused on educating, it now seems more interested in tapping into the same emotions as the viewer (Almeida, 2022; Bonsu et al., 2010). With the work of the new algorithms, we are given things that we already have an emotional affinity for, reducing our point of view to our own emotions on a subject. Symbolically speaking, it has shifted from creating a relationship between a teacher and a student with a clear hierarchy, as seen in PaleoTV, to a relationship between two equally restless students.

Television today, despite the existence of a (not always apparent) hierarchy, often prioritises the elicitation of emotional responses over the exchange of ideas. This tendency is reflected in the frequent use of aggressive language and reactive behaviour by the various figures and personalities. Rather than promoting constructive dialogue, modern television – as we have seen, depending on one's point of view, platforms such as YouTube and TikTok can be included in the traditional definition – seems more interested in cultivating a culture of emotional response, whether positive or negative, depending on the programme, time slot, or channel. This 'cult' seeks to evoke a collective emotional reaction from viewers, even though they are often mere observers on the other side of the screen or, in a sense, the other side of the mirror (Bradbury-Rance, 2023; Es, 2023; Faltesek et al., 2023).

However, as discussed, it is crucial that public service maintains its role as an 'open window' to the world, despite the challenges of our times. This requires not only resisting the aforementioned trends (of reflecting emotions) but also constantly seeking new solutions for programming and other challenges. It involves taking risks, being original, and breaking away from established norms. Constant service to the public is not – or should not be – constant subservience to the public. These, among other factors, render public service a perpetual challenge for all stakeholders – a challenge that, when measured against the yardstick of promoting responsible citizenship, will always prove to be a worthwhile endeavour. There is therefore no doubt that a Public Service 2.0 is needed, fully adapted to the new media environment and new means of communication. After all, it can only serve the public if it is present where the public is. But none of this can happen without first a certain sensitivity on the part of incumbent governments and then decisive action on their part to empower the media institutions themselves.

And there seems to be no doubt that people will increasingly inhabit the digital world. The new generations – coming of age, entering the workforce, building businesses, relationships, families, etc. – who have been accustomed to living in the digital world for as long as they can remember are increasingly occupying the human landscape of our planet. And undoubtedly, serving this new public, which is increasingly all of us, means being where the public is. And, ideally, anticipate where these people will be.

Television, as a human, social, and technological phenomenon, appears to be moving towards being less a specific technological object and more a media phenomenon diluted in many other objects of a technological nature. So, one thing seems clear: whatever the technological advances, television, more as a phenomenon than necessarily as an object, will adapt and, after some time, captivate us again and again.

At a time when *truth* has become secondary and the most important thing is to *truly communicate*, in many media solutions form is gradually replacing the role of content, and this really seems to be a trend for the future. A worrying trend, because practically everything we 'eat' in this new audiovisual environment seems to be already 'seasoned' with emotions, the emotions of others. We, as the general public, appear to have less and less freedom to purchase content free of emotions. Content that we can acquire and then, if we want, react emotionally (or not) based on our personal and social experiences.

But it seems important to remind media producers, especially for the future, that our human nature is capable of producing emotional responses. In fact, it is a sign of our vitality, of our individuality, that we are not machines, or rather that we have not been mechanised. We do not need, and it is not healthy for us as human beings, as consumers, as citizens, for everything to be soaked in emotion.

References

Almeida, A. (2022). *Daytime television in Portugal: An analysis of the role of laughter in the main morning talk shows* [Doctoral dissertation, Institute of Social Sciences, University of Minho]. http://repositorium.sdum.uminho.pt/handle/1822/75831

Bonsu, S., Darmody, A., & Parmentier, M. A. (2010). Arrested emotions in reality television. *Consumption Markets & Culture, 13*(1), 91–107. https://doi.org/10.1080/10253860903346781

Bradbury-Rance, C. (2023). 'Unique joy': Netflix, pleasure and the shaping of queer taste. *New Review of Film and Television Studies, 21*(2), 133–157. https://doi.org/10.1080/17400309.2023.2193521

Brandão, N. (2006). *[Prime time: What the TV news talks about] Prime time: do que falam as notícias dos telejornais*. Casa das Letras.

Brants, K. (1998). Who's afraid of infotainment? *European Journal of Communication, 13*(3), 315–335. https://doi.org/10.1177/0267323198013003002

Bustamante, E. (2003). *[The television economy: Media management strategies] A economia da televisão: as estratégias de gestão de um media* (L. Calapez, Trans.). Campo das Letras.

Charaudeau, P., & Ghiglione, R. (2000). *[The confiscated word – a television genre: the talk show] A palavra confiscada – um género televisivo: o talk show* (S. Azevedo, Trans.). Instituto Piaget.

Donders, K. (2019). Public service media beyond the digital hype: Distribution strategies in a platform era. *Media, Culture & Society, 41*(7). https://doi.org/10.1177/0163443719857616

Es, K. v. (2023). Netflix & Big Data: The strategic ambivalence of an entertainment company. *Television & New Media, 24*(6), 656–672. https://doi.org/10.1177/15274764221125745

Es, K., & Poell, T. (2020). Platform Imaginaries and Dutch Public Service Media. *Social Media + Society, 6*(2). https://doi.org/10.1177/2056305120933289

Faltesek, D., Graalum, E., Breving, B., Knudsen, E., Lucas, J., Young, S., & Zambrano, F. (2023). TikTok as Television. *Social Media + Society, 9*(3). https://doi.org/10.1177/20563051231194576

Fidalgo, J. (2005). [What do we talk about when we talk about public television service?] De que é que se fala quando se fala em serviço público de televisão? In M. Pinto (Ed.), *Televisão e cidadania: contributos para o debate sobre o serviço público* (2nd ed., pp. 23–40). Campo das Letras.

Gonçalves, H., & Pires, H. (2005). [Advertising and the public television service (the RTP case). Contributions to a reflection] A publicidade e o serviço público de televisão (o caso RTP). Contributos para uma reflexão. In M. Pinto (Ed.), *Televisão e cidadania: contributos para o debate sobre o serviço público* (2nd ed., pp. 115–131). Campo das Letras.

Lipovetsky, G. (2007). *[Paradoxical happiness: An essay on the hyper-consumer society] A felicidade paradoxal: ensaio sobre a sociedade de hiperconsumo* (M. Machado, Trans.). Companhia das Letras.

Lopes, F (1999). *[Public Television Service: The crisis, identity and challenges] Serviço Público de Televisão: a crise, a identidade e os desafios*. Lisboa: I Congresso das Ciências da Comunicação.

Lopes, F., Burnay, C., Santos, C., Santos, F., Wemans, J., Romano, R., & Silva, S. G. d. (2023). *[Public media service - White Paper] Serviço público de média - Livro branco*. Ministério da Educação e Ciência.

Maffesoli, M. (1998). *[The time of the tribes: The decline of individualism in mass societies] O tempo das tribos: o declínio do individualismo nas sociedades de massa* (M. Menezes, Trans.; 2nd ed.). Forense Universitára.

Maffesoli, M. (2001). *[The eternal instant: The return of the tragic in postmodern societies] O eterno instante: o retorno do trágico nas sociedades pós-modernas* (M. Figueiredo, Trans.). Instituto Piaget.

Maffesoli, M. (2014). *[Homo eroticus: Emotional communions] Homo eroticus: comunhões emocionais* (A. Chiquieri, Trans.). Forense.

Martins, M. (2005). [For a democracy to come. Public service television and civil society] Por uma democracia a vir. A televisão de serviço público e a sociedade civil. In M. Pinto (Ed.), *Televisão e cidadania: contributos para o debate sobre o serviço público* (2nd ed., pp. 7–10). Campo das Letras.

Pinto, M. (2005a). [Public service – a perspective] Serviço público – uma perspectiva. In M. Pinto (Ed.), *Televisão e cidadania: contributos para o debate sobre o serviço público* (2.a ed., pp. 11–21). Campo das Letras.

Pinto, M. (2005b). [Thinking and designing public service with public participation] Pensar e projectar o serviço público com a participação do público. In M. Pinto (Ed.), *Televisão e cidadania: contributos para o debate sobre o serviço público* (2nd ed., pp. 41–59). Campo das Letras.

Sousa, H. (1999). [Public service, commercial television and the implementation of the law: Some elements for the debate] Serviço público, televisão comercial e a implementação da lei: alguns elementos para o debate. *Comunicação e Sociedade, 1*, 121–130. https://doi.org/10.17231/comsoc.1(1999).1441

Sousa, H., & Santos, L. A. (2005). [RTP and public service: A journey of insurmountable dependence and contradiction] RTP e serviço público: um percurso de inultrapassável dependência e contradição. In M. Pinto (Ed.), *Televisão e cidadania: contributos para o debate sobre o serviço público* (2nd ed., pp. 61–80). Campo das Letras.

Stockwell, S (2004). *Reconsidering the fourth estate: The functions of infotainment.* APSA (Australian Political Studies Association) Conference.

Timberg, B. (2002). *Television talk: A history of the TV talk show.* University of Texas Press.

Torres, E. C. (2011). *[Television and public service] A televisão e o serviço público.* Fundação Francisco Manuel dos Santos.

Túñez-López, M., Campos-Freire, F., & Rodríguez-Castro, M. (Eds.). (2021). *The values of public service media in the Internet society.* Palgrave Macmillan.

Vasconcelos, A. (2003). *[Public service, private interests: What is at stake in the RTP controversy] Serviço público, interesses privados: o que está em causa na polémica da RTP.* Oficina do Livro.

Wolton, D. (1994). *[Praise of the general public: A critical theory of television] Elogio do grande público: uma teoria crítica da televisão* (M. Goucha, Trans.). Edições Asa.

Part II
Audiences

3 A New Era of Television

An Old Role for the Viewer

3.1 Yes, we are still the 'masses'

'Mass communication' is a complex and wide-ranging concept which encompasses the multifaceted, new and old phenomenon of television. As communication theorist McQuail (2003, p. 41) explains, the term is not new, having been used since the late 1930s. While the term 'masses' could once have been used positively, with connotations of collective strength and solidarity, in its early days it was typically associated with negative traits such as ignorance, violence, and lack of education. While we no longer associate it directly with social disorder, the negative view of the so-called 'masses' persists. McQuail suggests that this is because the term continues to be associated with ordinary people who lack education or refinement. Why? The author gives us an explanation: "The dominant social and cultural values in the 'West' have been individualistic and elitist, biased against collective action. (…) The word 'mass' also has unpleasant implications when applied to a group of people. It suggests an amorphous collection of individuals, without great individuality" (p. 41).

To reach the 'masses', one needs to use the so-called 'mass media' means of communication, which, though distinct in their own ways and in how they are received by the audience, share a common trait that they are intended and designed to reach many, explains McQuail (2003, p. 41). The relationship between sender and receiver, be it an organisation, journalist, politician, or other, is mediated by these means, resulting in a certain level of distance and impersonality. Moreover, despite any claims to the contrary, this relationship typically assumes a superior position over the anonymous and numerous viewers (Bradbury-Rance, 2023; Enns, 2021). As McQuail (2003) points out, "the relationship is not only asymmetrical, but also often calculating or manipulative in its intention, essentially non-moral" (p. 42), revolving around promising, requesting, or establishing some sort of unwritten contract, even if it does not impose any mutual legal obligations.

When it comes to the content produced and transmitted through these means, it is often not only reused but also repeated. The supposed 'innovation' is usually just a new packaging for a very old and familiar product that

DOI: 10.4324/9781003561675-6

moves towards a known end – profit. This profit, indirectly collected from the receiver, may or may not be financial and benefit the issuer or even the mediator. The aim is often to reach the largest audience with the lowest possible expense. According to McQuail (2003), this content "is essentially a commodity and differs in this respect from the content of other types of human communicative relationship" (p. 42).

In other words, the 'masses' are generally all of us, whether we like it or not. It is us as a collective. A collective that, in a given space (temporal or geographical), receives the same communication – the communication of the so-called mass media. And from the point of view of the mass media producers, we have more value collectively than individually. Having clarified this general concept and taking the recent and modern phenomenon of television as a concrete example, we can now approach the act of reception.

3.2   The public, the target, and the audience

In *Thinking Communication*, Wolton (1999, p. 414), the author, based on a reflection on public space, states that "the word public appears in the 14th century, from the Latin *publicus*, which refers to 'everyone'". The sociologist also suggests that the expression refers to something that is published, as in, that becomes public. On the other hand, the 'target' is reminiscent of the central circle into which arrows are thrown in a game (an image that appears in so many of the places associated with the name). Therefore, if the 'public' refers to all those whom the content can reach, then the 'target audience' refers to all those among them whom the content intends to reach.

The word 'audience' comes from the Latin word *audientia*, which in turn is derived from *audire* (to hear) and suggests more than simply acknowledging the existence of a sound. However, a large part of a 'target audience' may not be 'audience' in this sense, as doing so requires paying attention to the content. In ancient times, such as in Ancient Rome, requesting or providing an audience in theory meant that an individual or a collective would be heard or that they would listen attentively. The primitive concept of audiences is also evident in the Greco-Roman spectacles of yore, where the gathered crowds reacted by shouting, laughing, or even crying collectively to the performance. Although this primitive concept has similarities with the one explored here, such as being seen as a market, the modern audience, according to Denis McQuail (2003), differs in that it is "much larger and much more dispersed, individualized and privatized" (p. 365).

In the media industry, the term 'public' typically encompasses all those who have the potential to receive particular content, whether due to their geographical location or access to technology. On the other hand, the term 'target audience' refers to those for whom the content has been specifically designed. Meanwhile, 'audience' specifically refers to those who actually receive (watch or listen to) the content, regardless of whether they are part of the 'target audience' or not. To illustrate what has been said: if a particular programme only talks about football and its 'target audience' is all the lovers of that sport available in the vast and varied general 'public', the 'audience' refers only to those who have seen the programme (whether they like football or not).

Although these concepts belong to the past, they are still very relevant today. Whether it is national television, streaming solutions, or, in more amateur solutions, within personal channels on social media (Casado et al., 2023; Faltesek et al., 2023; Johnson, 2019; Podara et al., 2021; Sales, 2009; Wayne & Sandoval, 2023). More or less consciously, more or less used, they are still important from an economic perspective of the phenomenon, but also from an academic perspective. They are terms that are still part of the vocabulary and help us to better understand the phenomenon and its objectives and actions.

3.3 The imprecise – but crucial – calculation of audiences

On the topic of audiences, communication theorist McQuail (2003, p. 381) argues that it is crucial for media suppliers to have a precise understanding of their audience, both in terms of the size of the audience reached and the level of attention given, for financial, planning, and organisational reasons. As Torres (2011, p. 32) points out, "collectively, the spectators have power, and not negligible". While there may be occasional complaints about certain programmes, these views do not necessarily reflect the desires of the broader audience, which tends to be content with a narrow range of programming. However, if the goal is purely economic and focused on satisfying audiences, regardless of the potential negative effects, the question remains: how can one gauge the 'appetite' of audiences?

Traditional television audiences, along with many other types of audiences, cannot be known in absolute terms and are only estimated. However, these estimates have a significant impact on the real lives of audiences and are often immediately reflected in the programming that follows. For instance, in Portugal, the official methodology document (provided by GfK – Growth from Knowledge) uses a sample of 1,100 households representing the consumption of all individuals aged 4 or older residing in mainland Portugal, as outlined in the official methodology document (GfK, 2019). To better reflect Portuguese society, the sample is further subdivided into variables such as region, social class, households with subscriptions, and households without subscriptions. And something similar happens all over the world: a small sample is used to determine general interest. The collected data are then validated, weighted, and made available to the market. However, interpreting these data requires particular expressions and expertise in the field.

The *rating* is an estimate of the percentage of individuals who have watched a programme, while the *share* represents the percentage of viewers who watched that specific programme out of the total audience watching television at that time. For instance, if a programme had a rating of 20%, it means that approximately 20% of the population over the age of 4 have watched that programme. This value is crucial in determining advertising rates because it estimates the actual number of viewers who watched a given programme. On the other hand, if a programme has a share of 5%, it means that out of the 20% of the population watching television at that time, only 5% of viewers were watching that channel, while the remainder were tuned into other channels. But what changes does the future seem to bring to this still somewhat rudimentary mechanism for reading the social reality of audiences?

Although technological devices used to mediate these studies constantly progress at both hardware and software levels, the calculation of actual audiences remains, and will remain, impossible in an absolute sense due to numerous factors. As communication theorist Torres (2011, p. 66) stated, "quantitatively evaluating TV consumption completely is very difficult. TV signals 'fly' through the air, people's attention is dispersed, there are televisions turned on with no one paying attention to them, there is TV consumption outside the home or other equipment". An inaccuracy that is exacerbated by the introduction of new devices such as smartphones and tablets. It is unclear who exactly is watching and whether the phone or tablet belongs to the viewer. This is particularly relevant in the context of children when parents temporarily give their devices to their young children.

Not even the new advanced algorithms for the Internet context can really pinpoint the audience with absolute precision. It will always be an estimate. But despite their imprecise nature, this data is crucial for important decisions about content programming and channel management and serves as key indicators for determining advertising rates and other central aspects of the media industry. So, in truth, the so-called 'masses' and their 'tastes' are only estimated, not absolutely determined. And, therefore, it is not that rare for programmes to be discontinued despite having been the target of large investments. Something that happened in the past still happens today on modern television and will certainly continue to happen in the future to come. Television used to exist only because it had an audience. The same is true of television today. If there is one more certain truth about the future, it is that television will exist in the future only if there is an audience. So there is no doubt that measuring the size and tastes of that audience, however imprecisely, will be part of the future.

3.4   "Why am I here, watching this?" A question with no expiry date

"I'm watching this, but why this and not something else?" This simple question can cross any viewer's mind at some point or other, but its answer is of profound complexity. Therefore, a direct and absolutist explanation would be thoughtless and reckless. There are, however, some old theories that still offer some kind of explanation for this old, but still very topical question. McQuail and Windahl (2003), in their book *Communication Models for the Study of Mass Communication*, offer some insights on the topic "Reach, choice and appreciation of the audience" (pp. 130–137). While some of the theories discussed were not designed exclusively for television, new and old, they undoubtedly apply to this medium as well.

Let us start by examining the dissemination and (potential) reception of messages. In *The Mass Public at Grips with Mass Communications*, Clausse (1968) identified five dimensions of message reach. The first dimension encompasses all messages *distributed* through any means of communication at any time. The second dimension includes *receivable* messages, meaning all messages that can be received considering geographical and technological limitations. The third dimension includes only the messages that an individual *receives* because they are in a specific place at a specific time. The fourth dimension pertains to *recorded* messages, while the fifth dimension refers to the *internalised* message, which concerns the degree of attention and impact the message has on the viewer. Only in the final dimension of internalisation is the message truly stored in the mind of the receiver (Figure 3.1).

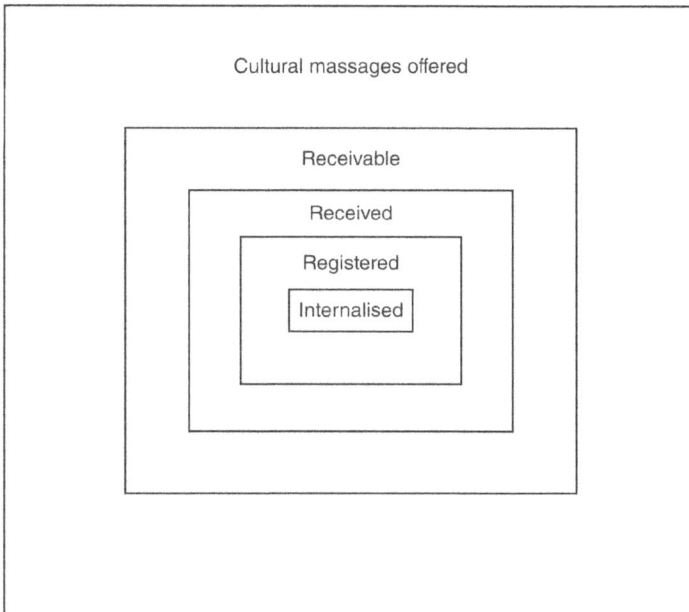

Cultural massages offered

Receivable

Received

Registered

Internalised

Figure 3.1 A tiny part of the existing message is received, and even smaller is the part that is internalised

Source: Clausse (1968, p. 632)

According to the theory under analysis, it is noteworthy that only a small portion of the available content actually reaches the viewer, and an even smaller fraction of that content is retained and internalised by the viewer. As a result, a significant amount of content is 'wasted' both by the media and by the viewers who are not watching the numerous other programmes available at the same time. Although the content is undoubtedly an essential part of the viewer's options, there are other factors that play a role in the decision to watch a programme, such as the viewer's availability and the programme's availability.

Taking this reality as a starting point and assuming a fixed programme structure, a free product, and an individual viewer, Webster and Wakshlag (1983), in *A Theory of Television Program Choice*, proposed a model for television programme choice that considers the individual viewer and the television industry's offer. They acknowledge that their model is, "at best, a tentative guide for deciphering paterns of program choice" (p. 443), as it depends on multiple factors. The first is the individual viewer and their availability, while the second factor is the television industry and its offer, and it is only from the convergence of these two variables that it is possible to analyse a set of other smaller, yet equally important nuances.

Denis McQuail (2003) based his own proposal on the model described by Webster and Wakshlag (1983), but expanded it to encompass all means of mass media, not just television (p. 397). And according to McQuail (2003, p. 397, 398), there are eight main factors (1–8) that explain the options of the *audience side*, and five aspects (A–E) that explain the choices of the *media side*. Although it may seem like an outdated model, it is not, as it still manages to be accurate, considering modern times and today's mass media.

On the audience side:

1 *Origin and social environment:* This includes habits influenced by social class, education, religion, and other factors that are often passed down through generations.
2 *Personal attributes:* This refers not only to personality but also to social position, age, level of education, and other individual characteristics.
3 *Media-related needs:* This refers to how viewers want to use media, whether for companionship, distraction, information, or other purposes.
4 *Personal tastes and preferences:* Viewers may seek out specific content based on their interests and preferences.
5 *General time use habits:* This includes factors such as availability, willingness, and financial resources to be part of a particular audience.
6 *Viewer's consciousness:* This refers to how viewers plan what they will watch based on the information they think they need.
7 *Specific context of use:* This includes the environment in which viewers are watching, such as whether they are alone or with others, which can influence their experience and choices.
8 *Chance:* Sometimes, chance is the only factor that can explain a viewer's choice.

On the media side:

a *System of media:* This refers to the available options, which can vary based on factors such as geographical location.
b *Structure of media supply:* This refers to the general pattern of expectations that media has created in their audiences over time.
c *Available content:* Depending on the time, location, and other factors, the content available to viewers can vary.
d *Advertising:* Media may use advertising for their own benefit, whether financial or otherwise, and this can affect the availability and pricing of specific content.
e *Opportunity and presentation:* Sometimes, exclusive content or a specific message is launched with the sole purpose of attracting viewers at a certain time.

As stated by McQuail (2003, p. 400), "the complexity and multiplicity of audience formation makes any simple description or single theoretical explanation difficult. We can certainly conclude that audiences are rarely what they seem". Despite this, it is possible to conclude that there are times when the interests of the media and audiences converge, even if not fully, thus providing a reasonable degree of satisfaction for both parties.

So, keeping in mind the initial question of 'why', the answer, though complex in its unfolding, ultimately is simple: *because both parties want it to be so.* And even today, it is never (only) the fault of the new algorithms. It is, then, with very few exceptions, always a 'communion' taken in mutual agreement. And it seems to be an answer not only for the present but also for the future: with no expiry date.

3.5   A future with a lot of past: The power of the *we* over the *I*

Although there is no consensus as to how and how much television is able to influence us, the truth is that all those who watch it, regardless of their level of education, age group, or other characteristics, inevitably end up indeed being affected by it. And, not infrequently, this force is exerted in such a diluted and apparently natural way that only a very attentive person is able to see that they are being directed by a force that is not, in totality, their own. People undeniably dress according to weather forecasts, give priority to products recommended by presenters, start sharing the same point of view of one of the many personalities, follow the recommendations of a health expert, visit a place or a space that has been suggested or shared with them, etc. And they do all this because they have seen or heard something about it on television. The only way not to be influenced by television is not to watch or listen to it. Otherwise, falling under some level of influence is inevitable. Obviously, television now shares its space with several other phenomena and devices, which was not the case before. However, it continues to influence us. It is part of its nature.

Prior to the 1930s, it was widely believed that mass media held 'all-powerful' influence, but by the 1950s, this view was challenged, and it was believed that the power of mass media was not as great as previously thought. However, with the emergence of television and other technological advances, there was a renewed discussion in the 1950s about the enormous power of mass media to shape society. By the 1970s, it became clear that the relationship between media and audiences was a negotiation. One that took place between the media and those receiving it. What can the past tell us about the present and the future? That in discussions about the media, especially here with regard to television, the focus is often not necessarily on its actual power but on the perception of that power. This perception can shift due to various factors, such as changes in technology or shifts in social attitudes, ultimately impacting the rhetoric surrounding the media (McQuail, 2003).

Nevertheless, it is possible that there are particular moments when the media are able to exert more or less influence on the viewers, regardless of the discourse that at that moment may involve them. Sudden and unforeseeable events, such as terrorist attacks, can drastically shift the power dynamic between the media and their audience. Denis McQuail (2003, p. 428) touches on this topic in his work, stating that "the power of the media can vary with the times". And we have seen this very clearly during the COVID-19 pandemic. Traditional television showed us all a social power that perhaps many of us had already forgotten it had (CAEM/MediaMonitor, 2021; Koivula et al., 2023). To fully comprehend the potential impact of the media on audiences, it is crucial to consider two key factors (which, although closely related, must also be observed separately): the prolonged discourse surrounding a particular topic and the influence of current and sometimes unexpected social events. These two variables are closely related yet distinct and require a deep understanding of the ever-changing reality that surrounds them, both spatially and temporally (McQuail, 2003).

On the other hand, with regard to the real effect of the media on our 'I', according to McQuail (2003, p. 430), there can be six main changes induced: (1) cause an intentional change; (2) cause an unintended change; (3) cause a minor change; (4) facilitate a change (whether or not it is desired); (5) reinforce the one that exists (including, and if applicable, no change); (6) and prevent or avoid a change. Obviously, the so-called 'effect' is also a variable dependent on a set of other aspects, which concern not only the media in general but also its receiver in particular, whether individual or collective.

Denis McQuail (2003, p. 432), influenced by Peter Golding's scheme, presents two important dimensions in the localisation of the effects of media on receptors: *intentionality* and *time*. According to such a scheme, the media can have several short-term effects, but it is in the long term that its influence can have a more significant impact on the life and routine of a viewer, altering not

only their reality but also their approach to it. Therefore, the choice of a programme by the viewer is not only a communion taken in mutual agreement,
but it is also an agreement executed continuously by both parties with regard
to the effect or power of the programme. In short, small changes can be sudden, of course, but according to the present reflection, the structural changes
of our *I* usually require more time from the media. This is because they are
changes that, although shared by television or any other media device, ultimately have the direct or indirect aim of shaping us. It is a modelling of our *I*
into a *We*, whatever it may be: political, ideological, religious, etc.

And there seems to be little – if any – difference between traditional television formats and the more modern ones to come. Whether they are amateur or
professional, local or global, it is the long exposure that brings long changes.
And the technology changes, but the role of the consumer remains the same:
to consume (Enns, 2021; Es, 2023).

Given that the new phenomenon of television, under the influence of the
Internet and even more so of artificial intelligence, has become increasingly
subtle in its ability to shape our ideas, directly or indirectly, should we also
increase our suspicion now and even more in the future? We will consider this
in the next topic.

References

Bradbury-Rance, C. (2023). 'Unique joy': Netflix, pleasure and the shaping of queer
taste. *New Review of Film and Television Studies, 21*(2), 133–157. https://doi.org/10
.1080/17400309.2023.2193521

CAEM/MediaMonitor. (2021). Total TV 2020 (YUMI Analytics Desktop).

Casado, M., Guimerà, J., Bonet, M., & Llavador, J. (2023). Adapt or die? How traditional Spanish TV broadcasters deal with the youth target in the new audiovisual ecosystem. *Critical Studies in Television, 18*(3), 256–273. https://doi.
org/10.1177/17496020221076983

Clausse, R. (1968). The mass public at grips with mass communications. *International
Social Science Journal, 20*(4), 625–643. https://unesdoc.unesco.org/ark:/48223/
pf0000024595

Enns, A. (2021). The illusion of control: History and criticism of interactive television.
Television & New Media, 22(8), 930–945. https://doi.org/10.1177/1527476420959770

Es, K. v. (2023). Netflix & Big Data: The strategic ambivalence of an entertainment company. *Television & New Media, 24*(6), 656–672. https://doi.
org/10.1177/15274764221125745

Faltesek, D., Graalum, E., Breving, B., Knudsen, E., Lucas, J., Young, S., & Zambrano, F. (2023). TikTok as television. *Social Media + Society, 9*(3). https://doi.
org/10.1177/20563051231194576

GfK. (2019). *[Methodology – audience measurement system] Metodologia – Sistema
de medição de audiências*. GfK.

Johnson, C. (2019). *Online TV*. Routledge.

Koivula, A., Räsänen, P., Marttila, E., Sedgwick, D., & Hawdon, J. (2023). COVID-19
compliance and media consumption: A longitudinal study of Finland and the US

during the first year of COVID-19. *Journal of Broadcasting & Electronic Media, 67*(4), 530–552. https://doi.org/10.1080/08838151.2023.2226276

McQuail, D. (2003). *[Mass communication theory] Teoria da comunicação de massas* (C. Jesus, Trans.). Fundação Calouste Gulbenkian.

McQuail, D., & Windahl, S. (2003). *[Communication models for the study of mass communication] Modelos de comunicação: para o estudo da comunicação de massas* (F. Cascais, Trans.). Editorial Notícias.

Podara, A., Matsiola, M., Kotsakis, R., Maniou, T., & Kalliris, G. (2021). Generation Z's screen culture: Understanding younger users' behaviour in the television streaming age - The case of post-crisis Greece. *Critical Studies in Television, 16*(2), 91–109. https://doi.org/10.1177/17496020211005395

Sales, M. (2009). The future of television: From the boob tube to YouTube. *American Communication Journal, 11*(1).

Torres, E. C. (2011). *[Television and public service] A televisão e o serviço público.* Fundação Francisco Manuel dos Santos.

Wayne, M., & Sandoval, A. (2023). Netflix original series, global audiences and discourses of streaming success. *Critical Studies in Television, 18*(1), 81–100. https://doi.org/10.1177/17496020211037259

Webster, J., & Wakshlag, J. (1983). A theory of television program choice. *Communication Research, 10*(4), 430–446. https://doi.org/10.1177/009365083010004002

Wolton, D. (1999). *[Thinking communication] Pensar a comunicação* (V. Anastácio, Trans.). Difel.

4   The Future of Television
What Awaits Us?

4.1   Its old companion, our new control, and artificial intelligence

Television can and should play a vital role in shaping citizens and building a more altruistic society, as we have discussed. However, the current trend towards commercialisation seems to be moving it in the opposite direction. In this sense, apart from (ideally) public service, what generally binds television to the viewer is not an altruistic interest in doing more and better, although that may exist, but undoubtedly its own survival. It can therefore be a relationship that is ultimately based on deeply 'selfish' interests on the part of television producers and that cultivates an inevitably 'calculative' relationship.

What happens then between television and its respective audiences, from this point of view, is, in the words of McQuail (2003, p. 367), "a transaction of money between producer and consumer rather than a communicative relationship". This problem is not limited to television alone, as sociologist Pierre Bourdieu (2001, p. 61) argues in *On Television*. He suggests that anything intermediated or influenced by television can gradually become influenced by it. Over time, these actors become burdened with the same economic and audience-related issues that plague television itself. And this is undoubtedly a reality that leads many people to have a negative view of television as a possible faithful companion.

If we rely on the suspicions of theorist Postman (2006) in *Amusing ourselves to death*, we can then see television as something that, while entertaining audiences, alienates them and is also capable of happily leading them into the abyss without them even being aware. From this perspective, television is seen as contributing to the oppression of its audiences by encouraging them to continue to be 'enamoured' with technology, despite the fact that it undermines their ability to think critically. This phenomenon can be seen as a kind of mesmerisation in which viewers are dazzled by a bright light that obscures their own mental clarity and independent thought.

However, according to Postman (2006, p. 87), the problem is not that television presents us with entertainment material, but that all content is presented

DOI: 10.4324/9781003561675-7

as entertainment, which is a completely different matter. In relation to this matter, and considering what television provides and what audiences require, the author argues that in the past, some religious leaders did not offer what people wanted but rather what they believed people needed. This shows that even at this level, television is now seen as something friendlier. Why? Unlike the religious leaders of the past, television is much easier to turn off (p. 121). Television that is switched off does not make money, and television that does not make money does not exist.

The thought under analysis is, in several respects, in tune with that of the theorist Theodor Adorno (2003), one of the best-known thinkers of the Frankfurt School. In the *Prologue on Television*, a reflection based on the studies he carried out while in America between 1952 and 1953, the author stated that television, "instead of conferring on the unconscious the honour of raising it to consciousness and thus allowing it to satisfy its impulses and pacify its destructive force" (p. 169), "reduces human beings more and more to their unconscious behaviours, when conditions give rise to an existence that threatens with suffering those who see through it and promise reward to those who idolize it" (p. 169). The theorist saw television at that time as an object of excellence, yes, but also as promoting the alienation of humans. Indeed, although he mentions that television may be the reproduction of an ancient desire of humanity, this in itself, he believes, does not mean that humanity is making the best of it. "Knowing how to desire correctly is the most difficult of the arts and we have discarded it since we left childhood" (p. 170), he said. Clearly, the author in question did not look kindly on television either. In fact, television has so far shown that it is an unfaithful, dubious, and even dangerous companion.

The Academy seems, from a very early age, in general, to have become accustomed to distrust the television phenomenon. Thus, this was a mistrust that naturally spread to countless other aspects and even to the very varied technological means of communication after television itself. As a phenomenon, television, especially in the beginning, was often presented as a kind of 'malignant tumour' of society, that is, something that needed to be continuously monitored, going so far as to understand that perhaps it should never have even existed. This assessment will certainly have often prevented television from being seen as a useful tool too.

As we will see below, it is not a question of whether television has been a faithful or unfaithful companion, but above all a question of focus, of perspective. For, depending on the 'lens' we use, television can be good or bad, faithful or unfaithful, pleasant or unpleasant, and it can be all of these at the same time.

When these dynamics are observed from the point of view of a ritual (based on James W. Carey), according to Denis McQuail (2003), "communication is not essentially instrumental or utilitarian, but normative. Audience members are essentially participants" (p. 381). From this perspective, the aim is for both the sender and the receiver to be viewed as participants in the same event, working together towards a common goal. Television, along with other media, is seen as a part of a larger social gathering and can be considered a 'competent' tool to fulfil a timeless human need for congregating. This is a view that brings us closer to the thinking of the so-called Chicago School and, consequently, to the "American pragmatism of John Dewey and George H. Mead" (Subtil, 2014, p. 21).

The French sociologist Dominique Wolton, among others, also argues in the opposite direction to the mainstream. In *Praise of the General Public*, Wolton (1994, p. 339) describes television as an important democratic instrument, a faithful, attentive, and consoling companion, a medium which, while capable of being a unifying instrument, does not cease to be an open window to the world, capable of presenting the viewer with the many and varied realities and events. "What, then, is the strength of television? Its popular success. And its weakness? The lack of legitimacy in the eyes of cultural elites" (Wolton, 2000, p. 55) summarises the same author in another book.

To the same extent that television continues to attract the so-called 'masses' by and large, it seems to continue to be rejected by cultural elites. Could it then be, at the heart of this old prejudice, a matter of jealousy? Perhaps. The elite's limited audiences are unlikely to provide the same level of quantitative attention as the vast and diverse audiences of television. And if this phenomenon was already evident in the past with general free-to-air television, it will be even more so now and in the future with streaming solutions and personal channels (YouTube, TikTok, etc.). But where do we stand? Is television, as a phenomenon rather than an object, a faithful or unfaithful companion for the future?

Television, as a social phenomenon, that is, as a social relationship, in terms of its company, can be whatever the recipient wants it to be, whether individual or collective. In fact, it is a relationship dependent on numerous variables, subordinated not only to television productions but also, in the collective sphere, with regard to its limits, to the State itself (the laws of a country or state). In addition, it is also delimited by the viewers, who can reduce, prolong, or completely cut off such a relationship at any time if they wish to do so.

The new and intelligent algorithms of the *new television* – which, as already analysed, can be extended to streaming platforms and social networks such as YouTube, TikTok, and the like – are moving us away from the generalist logic. Could this be bad? Undoubtedly, yes, because today's television, and by extension tomorrow's, increasingly seems to give us what we want to see, what we want to hear. So, if we lose the generalist value, which is a democratic value, we may lose the power to see the big picture. One of the big concerns that we seem to see very clearly for tomorrow's television and for media solutions in general is the fact that our overview is being reduced. Reduced to our emotional comfort.

We have the impression that we control what we watch on TV, whether it is traditional television, streaming platforms, YouTube, or similar services because we believe that we freely choose the content. On closer inspection, however, we may find that we are only watching what the producers want us to see. This is similar to the sense of control we felt when the remote control was introduced. We thought we were finally watching only what we wanted. In reality, this was an illusion because we could only watch what was available. Therefore, if at any point we believe we are in control, it is likely that we are mistaken and merely living an illusion of control (Enns, 2021; Esler, 2021). With the advent of artificial intelligence and algorithms that 'know' our preferences better than we do, this becomes even clearer. We are not seeing what we want; we are seeing what others want us to see – what others want to sell us. Television is undoubtedly easier and more accessible today (Johnson, 2019). But it is also more sinuous, making it harder to understand its real objectives.

Tomorrow's televisions will give us, according to the logic of algorithms, more and more of what *they* think is in our interests (within what is already in the interests of these large economic groups). This is undoubtedly dangerous. For us, for our critical spirit, for our society, for our social and democratic institutions. Rowing against the tide is undoubtedly an attempt to maintain the public service and, in one way or another, the generalist logic. This in no way hinders technological progress. But it can help to preserve our human and social nature in these days of enormous technological progress.

4.2   Looking for an increasingly open relationship

We will begin this section by primarily evoking the notion of *habitus,* proposed by sociologist Pierre Bourdieu (1997) in *Practical Reason.* The author, in this regard, stated: "one of the functions of the notion of *habitus* is to account for the unity of style that unites the practices and goods of a singular agent or a class of agents" (p. 9). In practical terms, and also according to his words, it is about what "the worker eats and above all his way of eating, the sport he practices and his way of practicing it" (p. 9). "The *habitus* are differentiated; but they are also differentiating" (p. 9). "They introduce different principles of differentiation or use common principles of differentiation differently" (p. 9). It is, therefore, a common practice, routine, but also identarian, which at the same time equalises some and differentiates others. A concept that, according to Pinto (2000, p. 45), also includes television practice.

Among other aspects, Pinto (2000, p. 45), in *Television in children's daily lives,* also noted that "while it is true that lifestyles are diverse, it is equally logical that there should be different ways of watching and using television" (p. 45). A myriad of *nuances,* at various levels, then shape the way individuals relate to television. And in this sense, based on the daily consumption of television by children, the researcher, illustrating, indicated that these data are variable according to the region, among other aspects. At one point, for example, children in the United States watched an average of four to six hours of television a day, compared with just over two hours a day in Europe (p. 144). Television consumption, as analysed, is therefore a social variable. But not only social, but also personal. During his fieldwork, for example, the author found that some children found a certain comedian funny and others did not. Some said they laughed at what the comedian said, others did not, saying they did not find it funny (p. 263). These are just two outstanding examples of many others that could be used to explain the phenomenon.

But what has changed in this social and personal habit in general? Perhaps the most obvious is the fact that, unlike in the past when television was the 'king' of the media and had virtually all the attention to itself, it now has to share that attention with dozens of other devices or other media content solutions. Viewers are therefore symbolically demanding a more open relationship with television. In other words, they do not just want to watch television; they *also* want to watch television, and that is very different. And they often do so while interacting on social networks, reading the news, or shopping. But it is not only the symbolic aspect that is changing; it is also the 'physical relationship' as an object (the logic of consumption), because now it is possible to watch television and at the same time fiddle with a smartphone, tablet, computer, etc., something that did not happen (comfortably) in the past with the radio, for example.

However, it is not only between devices and content solutions that television has to divide its attention, but now and increasingly in the future also between its own variables. This content can come from generalist television, thematic channels, new streaming solutions, or even increasingly popular and sophisticated personal channels, assuming that YouTube, TikTok, and other social networks that focus on the audiovisual image can be included in a television 2.0.

What can we expect in the future? More gadgets, certainly, more things to take our attention away from television. But ironically or not, the same devices that have taken attention away from television have also taken television to new heights: for example, we can now watch television on the bus, on the train, or on our smartphones. So perhaps television has not lost its former dominance but has shared it. A sharing that will surely extend to more and more devices in the future.

4.3 Celebrities cult: Will television still be a pedestal?

Postmodern theory, as explained by sociologist Giddens (2008), posits that the world has not become socialist as Marx had hoped but rather has been "dominated by the new media, which 'take us away' from our past" (p. 676). This view suggests that it is this same 'machine' that has created the new 'deities' known as 'celebrities', who are often idolised by many. These characters are constructed and presented by the media and their numerous human actors, but they can also be deconstructed and stripped down, as explained by Lins et al. (2017).

The media often presents real people in a filtered way, often creating an image of them that is different from reality. As a result, viewers may feel either a strong affinity or a strong dislike towards the character portrayed (and, indirectly, towards the person playing it). A number of 'mediators' are involved in this process, and new phenomena are emerging, but traditional television undoubtedly continues to play a particularly important role in this specific aspect of contemporary society. Think, for example, of world leaders and how many of them we do not know mainly through traditional television.

However, if we doubt this natural and real feeling towards a distant character, let us remember, among countless other possible examples, the case of Princess Diana. Giddens (2008, p. 677) explains that the Princess existed for the majority of people only through the media. Despite this, many did not inhibit themselves from mourning or lamenting her loss. Certainly, these countless people were not only crying for Diana, but above all for a character that she had played in the media for a long time. While people around the world mourned mainly the death of a character, family members wept for those who have played this role for so long. A significant difference that goes unnoticed by many.

But is this a thing of the past? Absolutely not. It still happens on new streaming platforms, and even more so on some personal Internet channels (YouTube, TikTok, etc.), where people become emotionally attached without really knowing the person behind the character. But take the recent case of Queen Elizabeth II. In general, her image was placed on a character for whom it was possible to have more empathy and more emotional affection (Tutan, 2023). This obviously makes it easier for the public to admire the person. But this shaping of perspectives affects not only people but also concepts that we can easily ignore or not even notice (Bradbury-Rance, 2023; Castelló, 2023). So, television can still sometimes put not only people on pedestals but also concepts and visions.

We speak of a new era with new great symbolic figures who, filtered by the media in general, are then deified and idolised by a significant part of society. These figures often, by their actions and their words, drive some people not only to act but also to react emotionally, laughing or crying at their mercy.

If traditional television was the main pedestal in the past, it is now, of course, just another pedestal. But it seems to be one that will continue for years to come, even more so if we assume that platforms such as YouTube and TikTok can be considered the television 2.0. If that is the case, then we can say without a doubt that television will certainly continue to be one of the main 'pedestals' of the future. But something is different, and it seems to be changing more and more. If in the past it was third parties who chose the 'celebrities' (the so-called TV experts), today, and even more so in the future, the choice will be made by the consumer. Many of these people are now moving from their personal social media channels to traditional television and also new streaming solutions. And why? Because they attract people, and not because they have the traditional training to work in television. Increasingly, it will be the consumer who puts a particular figure on a pedestal, based on their emotional connection rather than on what someone else has decided. We are talking about a collective and popular choice of the masses, as opposed to a choice made by an elite. In truth, in these cases, it is often an exercise in the subordination of elites to popular choices.

As Nietzsche pointed out, it is the 'modern people' who choose their 'gods' today and in the future, not the past and its leaders (Foucault, 1970; Nietzsche, 1996, 2001, 2005). The television of the future will therefore, based on this idea, be increasingly a cut with the past and what was the past, and increasingly a connection with the present, the emotions of the present (Baudrillard, 1994; Lourenço, 2006; Nietzsche, 1978).

4.4   The (re)connection: Old social needs with a long future?

Based on the reflection above about the 'veneration' of television deities, can we draw a comparison between television consumption and religious practices, both primitive and modern? To explore this comparison, we can start by examining the two main ideas behind the etymology of the word 'religion'. The first idea, proposed by Roman theorist Cicero (106-43 BC), many years ago, suggests that the word originates from *relego*, meaning to '(re)read', and therefore, according to him, religious practices encourage repeated absorption of the same content (Cícero, 2004, p. 92). The second idea, proposed by Augustine of Hippo (354-430 AD) centuries later, suggests that religion aims to '(re)connect' us with a connection lost since the Garden of Eden, encouraging a permanent attempt to recover that connection (Hipona, 2012, p. 195).

Despite the argument that television's success could be attributed to its attempt to fulfil an old human need, it is essential to consider another factor: the human need for 'logic' (from the Greek *logos*) or reason. As Durkheim (2002) highlighted in *The Elementary Forms of Religious Life*, people need "not only a sufficient moral conformism, but there is also a minimum of logical conformism that they cannot dispense with" (p. 20). And what about that particular aspect? Interestingly, or not, television is uninterruptedly committed to filling it as well.

Television productions not only try to create routines around entertainment but also propose (although they may obviously not fully comply with them) solutions for the fulfilment of logic, information, truth, and stability. As the researcher Lopes (2005, p. 99), "television is fundamentally guided by the vectors 'inform' and 'entertain'". And it is the existence of these two pillars, intertwined as one, that seems to have underpinned the unique success of traditional television in the past and continues to do so today.

Television encourages the viewer to see something repeated, both in terms of ideas and forms, and also encourages people to make a continuous effort to try to resume a connection that, for some reason and for some time, may be corrupted. As for the goal of the viewer, it is to continually try to understand what they are seeing, coming from the curiously titled 'vision of the beyond' (from *tele* and *vision*), that is, of television. Many of the audiences' choices are also anchored, by numerous personal and social factors, to specific television channels, as if it were a religious entity – their own entity. And their attachment, at times, in the sight of others, is something seemingly irrational. The success and progress of television are unique, and the need for society to coexist with this phenomenon is truly fascinating. But is it then feasible to compare the exercise of television to a religious practice? Are we, in this small topic, unravelling a mystery? Although there are some points in common in these two fields, this is an extremely complex issue, requiring a broader and deeper reflection at various levels, which is completely unenforceable at this time for numerous reasons.

But one thing seems certain: if there is harmony between these two concepts, it only proves that television – less as an object than as a concept – has a future, a great future. Nevertheless, let us note, in the last topic, the idea of 'ritual' – something that, although it also underlies religious practice, is not at all exclusive to it.

4.5   What kind of future can we expect?

"It would have been better to come back at the same hour", said the fox. "If, for example, you come at four o'clock in the afternoon, then at three o'clock I shall begin to be happy. I shall feel happier and happier as the hour advances. At four o'clock, I shall already be worrying and jumping about. I shall show you how happy I am! But if you come at just any time, I shall never know at what hour my heart is to be ready to greet you... One must observe the proper rituals..."

"What is a ritual"? asked the little prince.

"Those also are actions too often neglected", said the fox. "They are what make one day different from other days, one hour from other hours".

(Saint-Exupéry, 2008, p. 70)

Saint-Exupéry said that rituals are important, as he explains through his character, *the fox*. But sometimes people can distract themselves from this reality, as Saint-Exupéry's character also suggests. Television, old and new versions, on the other hand, according to Lopes (2005), needs this reality all the time to distract us, something quite different. For example, Lopes describes television as a 'totem' that creates a permanent emotional bond with its viewers and serves as a companion in different situations, establishing a ritual with its own names and symbols (p. 81). This larger 'ritual' prompts viewers to perform a set of minor tasks that are equally constant within themselves.

Before we embark on this path, it is impossible not to mention the well-known communication theorist James W. Carey (1988), who drew our attention to a ritualistic perspective of communication. While the initial models of mass communication depicted a linear and one-way relationship between the sender and the receiver, the American theorist introduced a new approach. The author points to the focus "not the act of imparting information or influence but [rather for] the creation, representation, and celebration of shared even if illusory beliefs" (p. 43).

According to this perspective, as McQuail and Windahl (2003), communication relies on shared interpretations and emotions, with its objectives leaning towards festivity, consumerism, and decoration rather than utility (p. 52). And yet, according to Subtil (2014), "ritual vision of communication derives from a conception of religion that dismantles the role of the sermon, instruction and warning, and that highlights the small activities of everyday life, the feast, the song and the prayer" (p. 28). In light of this perspective, it is a matter of likening the act of communication, be it television or otherwise, new or old, to an almost unconscious religious habit rather than a conscious and reflective practice of religiosity.

From this perspective, television, now and in the future, can be viewed as a medium that 'only' attempts to fulfil a fundamental human and social need, namely the desire to connect with others through shared beliefs and narratives. In the past, people would regularly gather around campfires to hear stories of all kinds – from comedy to tragedy to true or fantastical tales– and, argues Robert A. White (1994) in *Television as Myth and Ritual,* people still gather in much the same way around television. The act of coming together and the underlying need to do so remain unchanged; only the appearance of the gathering has evolved into its most modern form. Maffesoli (1995) describes this phenomenon as follows: "television allows to 'vibrate' in common. One weeps, one laughs, one taps in unison, and thus, without really being in the presence of others, a kind of communion is created" (p. 77).

According to this view, there seems to be little doubt as to the fact that, in the television phenomenon, new and old, there is an invisible link that has a very real presence which is capable of 'uniting' all those who watch any television programme at the same time. We used to watch television programmes at exactly the same time, but with new streaming services, new televisions that allow us to watch programmes again, and even online channels (YouTube, TikTok, etc.), this connection time has increased. It could be a week, a month, or more. But sooner or later, when we watch the same programme, the same film, the same series, and the same content as the people around us, and we talk about it, it creates connections in us. Or rather, it creates a reason and a possible motivation to connect with each other.

However, for Wolton (1994, p. 142), in addition to gathering, television and society are united in yet another aspect: television, as a mirror of society, thus equally offers it "a representation [of itself]". The author continues: "Television creates not only an image and a representation of it but offers a connection to all who see it at the same time. It is, in fact, one of the only instances in which this society is reflected, while at the same time allowing everyone to access this representation".

The way in which viewers relate to television is constantly changing and influenced by various factors. Today, we can clearly observe a reinterpretation of the traditional concept of 'television', which is increasingly detached from the old television set and the old way of producing television content (Casado et al., 2023; Faltesek et al., 2023; Johnson, 2019; Podara et al., 2021; Sales, 2009; Wayne & Sandoval, 2023). However, throughout its history, television has continued to fulfil the ancient human need to gather and share common beliefs. This suggests that the lack of human connection is a permanent phenomenon that will continue into the future, and television (as a phenomenon rather than as a device) will certainly continue to try to exploit this lack with new mechanisms and strategies.

Society has become accustomed to television as a phenomenon, just as it has become accustomed to the need for many other things that are still very much alive today. It may therefore be premature to assume that even traditional television, the generalist with an open signal, is dead or dying. Traditional television is still very much alive today, in many places and for many people, and its social role is also very much alive (CAEM/MediaMonitor, 2021; ERC, 2016). It would be as foolish to declare a television dead or dying without careful examination as it would be during a rescue operation to assume that a body is not alive without thorough examination. Let us not be blinded by the unfounded and 'prophetic' statements from those who have been announcing the death of television for decades. If we fall for such claims, we might miss the crucial point of how television can still be useful and where the phenomenon is headed (Enns, 2021; Esler, 2021; Hagedoorn et al., 2021).

Society is different: increasingly hostage to its emotions, increasingly eager to feel, to feel different things, and to share these feelings (Maffesoli, 2001). Television, as a social mirror, not only reflects this reflection but also influences it (Bartsch, 2012; Bonsu et al., 2010). Because now the people in front of it are also different (Hochschild, 2012; Lipovetsky, 2007; Maffesoli, 1995, 2001, 2014; Martin, 2011). So, in general, television has no choice but to reflect the body in front of it. Do we sometimes wish that our bodies in front of the mirror were different? Yes, we do. Is that possible? Not at all. The image we see is not always the image we would like to see, both personally and socially.

So, we are not referring to social ideals, whatever they may be and whatever ideas they may be anchored in, but to social reality. This is what television will always reflect, more or less clearly: the values, beliefs, and dreams of the moment.

If, in the past, the social stage was mainly about connecting ideas, today, in (post)modern societies, it seems to be mainly about seeking emotional connections, with fewer social boundaries and more personal ones (Almeida, 2024b; Giddens, 1992; Lourenço, 2006; Maffesoli, 2001). Therefore, it is not surprising that members of this *new society* utilise the mechanisms that surround them to connect emotionally. However, it is important to note that television is not just any mechanism; it is one of the oldest in this field of mass communication and one of the most familiar, with which society feels most comfortable. In other words, without shame in showing *nudity*, without fear or hesitation in showing its intentions.

In short, how do today's televisions generally satisfy their general audience? The answer is not to give them emotions. It is something more complex: give them their emotions. Or even more complex: give them rituals (routines) with their own emotions. And this trend increasingly seems to be growing for a future yet to come, where everything indicates that television will be less and less about ideas and more and more about emotions. Less is more. We learn. But in this particular case, it is doubtful.

It is true that emotions and popular communication can be useful as a form of soft literacy in democratic and social dynamics, contributing to the development of society itself (Almeida, 2024a, 2024c; Almeida & Wolton, 2024). Here, however, the focus is different: television is predominantly becoming just that. In fact, the media in general, reflecting contemporary society, are becoming predominantly emotional and popular. The exclusive emphasis on an emotional and popular discourse overlooks that there is also a less popular and emotional side to society. Or at least there should be, if it is to function properly. For not everything in our societies is very good or very bad. Not everything is emotional. There is a place that is normal, grey, and lukewarm where emotions are not even welcome.

References

Adorno, T. (2003). [Prologue on Television] Prólogo sobre a televisão (M. Resende, Trans.). In *Sobre a indústria da cultura* (pp. 161–171). Angelus Novus.

Almeida, A. (2024a). Daytime television in Portugal: A look at the evolution of morning talk shows (1985-2023). *Observatorio (OBS*)*, *18*(2), 99–118. https://doi.org/10.15847/obsOBS18220242370

Almeida, A. (2024b). Do societies have emotions? *Societies*, *14*(5), 65. https://doi.org/10.3390/soc14050065

Almeida, A. (2024c). Praising pop emotions: Media emotions serving social interests. *Humanities and Social Sciences Communications*, *11*(1), 757. https://doi.org/10.1057/s41599-024-03210-2

Almeida, A., & Wolton, D. (2024). The role of television in shaping democracy: An old dream with a big future? *Comunicação e Sociedade*, *45*, e024007. https://doi.org/10.17231/comsoc.45(2024).4893

Bartsch, A. (2012). Emotional gratification in entertainment experience. Why viewers of movies and television series find it rewarding to experience emotions. *Media Psychology, 15*(3), 267–302. https://doi.org/10.1080/15213269.2012.693811

Baudrillard, J. (1994). *Simulacra and simulation* (S. F. Glaser, Trans.). University of Michigan Press.

Bonsu, S., Darmody, A., & Parmentier, M. A. (2010). Arrested emotions in reality television. *Consumption Markets & Culture, 13*(1), 91–107. https://doi.org/10.1080/10253860903346781

Bourdieu, P. (1997). *[Practical Reason. On the theory of action] Razões práticas: sobre a teoria da acção* (M. Pereira, Trans.). Celta Editora.

Bourdieu, P. (2001). *[On Television] Sobre a televisão* (M. Pereira, Trans.). Celta Editora.

Bradbury-Rance, C. (2023). 'Unique joy': Netflix, pleasure and the shaping of queer taste. *New Review of Film and Television Studies, 21*(2), 133–157. https://doi.org/10.1080/17400309.2023.2193521

CAEM/MediaMonitor. (2021). Total TV 2020 (YUMI Analytics Desktop).

Carey, J. W. (1988). *Communication as culture: Essays on media and society.* Routledge.

Casado, M., Guimerà, J., Bonet, M., & Llavador, J. (2023). Adapt or die? How traditional Spanish TV broadcasters deal with the youth target in the new audiovisual ecosystem. *Critical Studies in Television, 18*(3), 256–273. https://doi.org/10.1177/17496020221076983

Castelló, E. (2023). Voices from the emptiness. Developing the agentic rural on Spanish television. *Critical Studies in Television.* https://doi.org/10.1177/17496020231202511

Cícero. (2004). *[Of the nature of the gods] Da natureza dos deuses* (P. Falcão, Trans.). Vega.

Durkheim, É. (2002). *[The elementary forms of religious life: The totemic system in Australia] As formas elementares da vida religiosa: o sistema totémico na Austrália* (M. Pereira, Trans.). Celta Editora.

Enns, A. (2021). The illusion of control: history and criticism of interactive television. *Television & New Media, 22*(8), 930–945. https://doi.org/10.1177/1527476420959770

ERC. (2016). *[The new dynamics of audiovisual consumption in Portugal] As novas dinâmicas do consumo audiovisual em Portugal.* ERC.

Esler, M. (2021). In plain sight: Online TV interfaces as branding. *Television & New Media, 22*(7), 727–742. https://doi.org/10.1177/1527476420917104

Faltesek, D., Graalum, E., Breving, B., Knudsen, E., Lucas, J., Young, S., & Zambrano, F. (2023). TikTok as Television. *Social Media + Society, 9*(3). https://doi.org/10.1177/20563051231194576

Foucault, M. (1970). *The order of things: An archaeology of the human sciences* (R. D. Laing, Ed.). Pantheon Books.

Giddens, A. (1992). *The transformation of intimacy: Sexuality, love, and eroticism in modern societies.* Stanford University Press.

Giddens, A. (2008). *[Sociology] Sociologia* (A. Figueiredo, A. Baltazar, C. d. Silva, P. Matos, V. Gil, Trans.; 6thed.). Fundação Calouste Gulbenkian.

Hagedoorn, B., Eichner, S., & Lozano, J. (2021). The 'youthification' of television. *Critical Studies in Television, 16*(2), 83–90. https://doi.org/10.1177/17496020211011804

Hipona, A. d. (2012). *[The true religion] A verdadeira religião* (P. Silva, M. Ramos, Trans.). Edições Afrontamento.

Hochschild, A. R. (2012). *The managed heart: commercialization of human feeling*. University of California Press.

Johnson, C. (2019). *Online TV*. Routledge.

Lins, A., Oliveira, M., & Santos, L. (2017). [Body figurations in the spontaneous of digital photojournalism: The non-pose and disfiguration] Figurações de corpo no espontâneo do fotojornalismo digital: a não-pose e a desfiguração. *Comunicação e Sociedade, 32*, 399–417. https://doi.org/10.17231/comsoc.32(2017).2769

Lipovetsky, G. (2007). *[Paradoxical happiness: An essay on the hyper-consumer society] A felicidade paradoxal: ensaio sobre a sociedade de hiperconsumo* (M. Machado, Trans.). Companhia das Letras.

Lopes, F. (2005). [The contents of the public television service: Clues for the elaboration of a programming grid] Os conteúdos do serviço público de televisão: pistas para a elaboração de uma grelha de programação. In M. Pinto (Ed.), *Televisão e cidadania: contributos para o debate sobre o serviço público* (2nd ed., pp. 81–114). Campo das Letras.

Lourenço, E. (2006). [In the shadow of Nietzsche] À sombra de Nietzsche. In C. d. Sousa, J. d. Lima (Eds.), *Heterodoxias* (Vol. 1). Fundação Calouste Gulbenkian.

Maffesoli, M. (1995). *[The contemplation of the world] A contemplação do mundo* (F. Settineri, Trans.). Artes e Ofícios.

Maffesoli, M. (2001). *[The eternal instant: The return of the tragic in postmodern societies] O eterno instante: o retorno do trágico nas sociedades pós-modernas* (M. Figueiredo, Trans.). Instituto Piaget.

Maffesoli, M. (2014). *[Homo eroticus: Emotional communions] Homo eroticus: comunhões emocionais* (A. Chiquieri, Trans.). Forense.

Martin, J. (2011). *Between heaven and mirth: Why joy, humor, and laughter are at the heart of the spiritual life*. HarperOne.

McQuail, D. (2003). *[Mass communication theory] Teoria da comunicação de massas* (C. Jesus, Trans.). Fundação Calouste Gulbenkian.

McQuail, D., & Windahl, S. (2003). *[Communication models for the study of mass communication] Modelos de comunicação: para o estudo da comunicação de massas* (F. Cascais, Trans.). Editorial Notícias.

Nietzsche, F. (2001). *The gay science* (J. Nauckhoff, B. Williams, Ed.). Cambridge University Press.

Nietzsche, F. (1978). *Thus spoke Zarathustra* (W. Kaufmann, Trans.). Penguin Books.

Nietzsche, F. (1996). *Human, all too human: A book for free spirits* (R. J. Hollingdale, Trans.). Cambridge University Press.

Nietzsche, F. (2005). Twilight of the idols or how to philosophize with a hammer [Turin, on 30 September 1888] (J. Norman, A. Ridley, J. Norman (Eds.), *The Anti-Christ, Ecce Homo, Twilight of the Idols, and other writings* (pp. 153–229). Cambridge University Press.

Pinto, M. (2000). *[Television in children's daily lives] A televisão no quotidiano das crianças*. Edições Afrontamento.

Podara, A., Matsiola, M., Kotsakis, R., Maniou, T., & Kalliris, G. (2021). Generation Z's screen culture: Understanding younger users' behaviour in the television streaming age - The case of post-crisis Greece. *Critical Studies in Television, 16*(2), 91–109. https://doi.org/10.1177/17496020211005395

Postman, N. (2006). *Amusing ourselves to death: Public discourse in the age of show business*. Penguin Books.

Saint-Exupéry, A. D. (2008). *[The little Prince] O principezinho* (J. M. Varela, Trans.; 29th ed.). Editorial Presença.

Sales, M. (2009). The future of television: From the boob tube to YouTube. *American Communication Journal, 11*(1).

Subtil, F. (2014). [James W. Care's cultural approach to communication] A abordagem cultural da comunicação de James W. Carey. *Intercom: Revista Brasileira de Ciências da Comunicação, 37*(1), 19–44. https://doi.org/10.1590/S1809-58442014000100002

Tutan, D. (2023). Simulating the past in the present through biopics: Queen Elizabeth II on screen and on TV. *Journal of Popular Film and Television, 51*(2), 73–83. https://doi.org/10.1080/01956051.2023.2180615

Wayne, M., & Sandoval, A. (2023). Netflix original series, global audiences and discourses of streaming success. *Critical Studies in Television, 18*(1), 81–100. https://doi.org/10.1177/17496020211037259

White, R. A. (1994). [Television as myth and ritual (Part 1)] Televisão como mito e ritual (1.a parte). *Comunicação & Educação*, (1), 47–55. https://doi.org/10.11606/issn.2316-9125.v0i1p47-55

Wolton, D. (1994). *[Praise of the general public: A critical theory of television] Elogio do grande público: uma teoria crítica da televisão* (M. Goucha, Trans.). Edições Asa.

Wolton, D. (2000). *[And after the Internet? Towards a critical theory of new media] E depois da internet? Para uma teoria crítica dos novos médias* (R. Branco, Trans.). Difel.

The Television of Tomorrow
A (Non) Conclusion

Television, once seen as a window to the world, a platform for presenting the diverse and unimaginable aspects of our local or global society, is undergoing a remarkable transformation (Almeida & Wolton, 2024; Faltesek et al., 2023; Johnson, 2019; Lopes et al., 2023). Its original purpose was to enlighten and educate viewers, to offer insights into cultures, ideas, and realities often far removed from their own. Its aim was to act as a bridge between people and the world, opening their eyes to new horizons and promoting understanding of the human experience. In recent years, however, there has been a marked change in the fundamental nature of television. Its original purpose seems to be disappearing in the fog of the present, where emotions and commercialism are the main pillars.

Contemporary television seems to be increasingly concerned with a different goal – the relentless pursuit of emotional engagement. In general, the medium has ceased to be an educational tool and has become an emotional box. It uses sophisticated algorithms to personalise content, delivering exactly what viewers already have an emotional affinity for. As a result, the diversity of perspectives that television once championed has diminished, and its focus is now on feeding the same emotions that its audience already possesses. It seems to be a box of emotions from which the viewer selects only those he or she likes. This change symbolically transforms the relationship between the audience and the medium itself. The conventional structure, similar to the teacher-student dynamic of earlier forms of television, has now been transformed into a relationship between two equally emotional participants.

This shift in emphasis is evident in the widespread use of emotional language and reactive behaviour by various characters and personalities on television. Rather than promoting constructive dialogue and fostering a climate of critical thinking, modern television, which can be defined to include platforms such as YouTube and TikTok, seems more interested in cultivating a culture of emotional response.

In the context often referred to today as 'modern knowledge', also influenced by Darwinism and Spencerian thought, emotions are seen as merely the ancestors of what people now recognise as music (Darwin, 1859, 1871a,

DOI: 10.4324/9781003561675-8

1871b, 1872; Spencer, 1857, 1860). Without going into the details of this vision, but only with this general analogy in mind, one question inevitably arises for the media in general, and television in particular, from here into the future: what about silence – is it not also necessary, even in the process of appreciating music?

In the midst of these changes, however, it is vital that public service television continues to fulfil its traditional role as an *open window* to the world. To do this, public service must be innovative, take risks, and break with established norms. Commitment to the public should not be synonymous with subservience to popular trends, as it is vital to preserve the unique role of public service in promoting responsible citizenship. In the era of new media and communication channels, there is an urgent need for a Public Service 2.0, fully adapted to the evolving media landscape and able to meet the public where they are. Can we expect a public service that is not only present but active on platforms such as Netflix, HBO, YouTube, TikTok, and others? Can we expect a public service that is also increasingly capable of using new algorithms, but instead of giving us what we want, it gives us the opposite: other points of view, the contradictory? There are a number of aspects that need to be considered, promoted, and put into practice. It is necessary to (re)think a public service adapted to the new public.

If it were possible to define the television of the future in one sentence, it would be this, supported by this essay: *television will be less and less an object and more and more a phenomenon, that is, less and less a single object and more and more a phenomenon diluted in different objects.* What about television audiences in the future? *Audiences will demand an increasingly open relationship in which the attention once given only to television will be increasingly shared with other devices and phenomena of communication and interaction. They will no longer only want to watch television, but they will also want to watch television, which is something quite different.* In fact, this is already happening. But it seems to have become more apparent recently. As far as the concept of television is concerned, even the oldest is perfectly capable of accommodating all these changes. In fact, because it has been so broad since its creation, it seems to have been waiting for all these changes and others.

Television seems to be on its way to becoming a box of emotions that, once opened, will only give us what we already want, or think we want. And that is the danger: having only what we think we want. No society will be able to resist this in a healthy way if everyone gets used to satisfying only their own desires. The aim is not to dramatise what is happening and what seems to be the future of this phenomenon (and mass media in general), but simply to try to raise awareness of a trend that seems increasingly evident. Television, traditional or modern, as a unique audiovisual communication phenomenon, can and should continue to be an open window to the many worlds within this world and not a closed mirror of our own emotions. This means not becoming a decorative object in our society but being what it has always wanted to be, being what it has been: an important pillar of social and democratic values. It seems undeniable that television is now less a physical object, fixed in one place, and more a social phenomenon, accessible everywhere. But it is equally undeniable that it is now more of a box of emotions that we can access anywhere, and that it no longer functions, or functions less, as an open window through which to look out at the world. And to do this to television is to reduce its potential.

References

Almeida, A., & Wolton, D. (2024). The role of television in shaping democracy: an old dream with a big future? *Comunicação e Sociedade*, *45*, e024007. https://doi.org/10.17231/comsoc.45(2024).4893

Darwin, C. (1859). *On the origin of species by means of natural selection*. John Murray.

Darwin, C. (1872). *The expression of the emotions in man and animals*. John Murray.

Darwin, C. (1871a). *The descent of man, and selection in relation to sex* (Vol. 1). John Murray.

Darwin, C. (1871b). *The descent of man, and selection in relation to sex* (Vol. 2). John Murray.

Faltesek, D., Graalum, E., Breving, B., Knudsen, E., Lucas, J., Young, S., & Zambrano, F. (2023). TikTok as Television. *Social Media + Society*, *9*(3). https://doi.org/10.1177/20563051231194576

Johnson, C. (2019). *Online TV*. Routledge.

Lopes, F., Burnay, C., Santos, C., Santos, F., Wemans, J., Romano, R., & Silva, S. G. d. (2023). *[Public media service - White Paper] Serviço público de média - Livro branco*. Ministério da Educação e Ciência.

Spencer, H. (1857). The origin and function of music [October, 1857]. In *Fraser's magazine* (Vol. 56, pp. 396–408). John W. Parker and Son, West Strand Publisher.

Spencer, H. (1860). The physiology of laughter [March, 1860]. In D. Masson (Ed.), *Macmillan's magazine* (Vol. 1, pp. 395–402). Macmillan and Co.

Supplemental Topics
Methodology

The content presented was mostly supported by a *documentary analysis*. This analysis was particularly based on a *literature review*. As for the focus, this was mainly the exploration of some of the main concepts and problems of the television phenomenon. The so-called future, in this work, is nothing more than an idea — an idea supported by the sum of what was the past and what is the present of the phenomenon.

If, in your careful reading, you have found any appreciation that you have found reductive or even erroneous, please share it with me. The 'landscape' observed is always the result of a point of view, and this is inevitably limited, circumscribed, and nothing better than a call for attention to enlarge it, to enrich it. I will carefully examine the arguments and the shared bibliography and, where necessary, in future releases, adjust my perspective, thanking and crediting each of these precious remarks.

Acknowledgements

My thanks goes to my mother, Luciana, of course; secondly, to the editor who made this possible, Alice Salt, and thirdly, to my friends, all of them.

What Future Do We Want for Television?

by Dominique Wolton (edited by Abílio Almeida)

Television was the first mass communication medium after radio. In fact, television and radio are inseparable in a project of social emancipation. While the written press was undoubtedly important in establishing democracy, it primarily catered to the literate elite. Television, on the other hand, showed us that the masses could be democratic, regardless of literacy level, and was an open tool accessible to people from all social strata. The success of this long-forgotten project aimed at promoting democracy and mass communication is fascinating, and it is something that continues to interest me today.

The early visionaries of television and radio in the 1920s had a fascinating social project in mind: to educate, educate, educate, and entertain the public through a combination of leisure, politics, and civic awareness. This purpose was highly ambitious, and today we are more aware of its significance as we grapple with the individualism of the Internet. Television and radio programmes alike aimed to raise the cultural and intellectual bar for everyone.

Television fought for political independence from the government for years. However, now that this battle has been won, it is crucial not to overlook the ongoing struggle for financial independence. In essence, we must continue to strive towards this goal. This is a challenge that extends beyond just radio and television but also encompasses the Internet and all cultural and communication industries. Given the significant amount of money involved, so-called 'freedom' can easily become entangled with other interests, even if it appears to be preserved.

In today's Internet age, the governing principle seems to be individual freedom. However, it is important to recognise that the concept of individual freedom has been around since the 19th century. Our concern should not solely be about individual freedom but also emancipation. In the past, people regarded television as 'the school of the 20th century' although this may have been a slight exaggeration, it at least demonstrated a desire for ambition. However, with the rise of thematic television, and even more so with the Internet, we are witnessing the opposite movement take place: segmentation and individualisation. In other words, people may be interested in areas such as fishing, sex, or politics, but as a rule, there is no general incentive to broaden horizons. So, the first challenge is to preserve the logic of supply and the general interest.

Despite the plethora of technologies and programmes available today, many argue that we have reached an era of 'equality for all'. However, this could not be further from the truth. Programmes that cater to the entire population are almost non-existent, despite the abundance of choices. While the options may seem endless, they are not driven by a democratic spirit. Instead, there is widespread confusion between the concepts of 'citizen' and 'consumer'. It takes political will to maintain diversity in supply, which brings us to the need for a public service of media.

Regardless of what is said or done, it is only through a public service that interesting programmes, albeit with a smaller audience, may continue to exist. Unfortunately, the audience cannot be the only criterion, which is often the case. One lesson I learnt from my work is the danger of fragmentation. Therefore, it is in the interest of a public service to maintain a diverse offering for all, ensuring general interest is maintained. I believe that the values that underpinned the establishment of radio and television in the 1940s and 1960s are still relevant today. This is not surprising since society's core values do not change every 30 years. What changes every thirty years is the technique. Unfortunately, the rapid pace of technological change is perceived as a change in the nature of communication. But are different things.

It is up to those who work in the media to shift the current balance of power – the dominant ideology that favours the Internet over television. It is misguided to support one over the other because there is room for both. Television can do things that the Internet cannot, and vice versa. Today, you cannot have one without the other. They are often already one. Television is undoubtedly a crucial political challenge because it raises important questions for all of us about equality and democracy.

Dominique Wolton
CNRS, Paris, France

Index

For Product Safety Concerns and Information please contact our EU
representative GPSR@taylorandfrancis.com
Taylor & Francis Verlag GmbH, Kaufingerstraße 24, 80331 München, Germany

www.ingramcontent.com/pod-product-compliance
Lightning Source LLC
Chambersburg PA
CBHW071059280326
41928CB00050B/2566